PLANT-BASED COOKING

for
ABSOLUTE BEGINNERS

PLANT-BASED COOKING

for
ABSOLUTE BEGINNERS

60 Recipes & Tips for **Super Easy Seasonal Recipes**

THERESE ELGQUIST

Translated by Gun Penhoat

Skyhorse Publishing

Translation copyright © 2021 by Skyhorse Publishing
Copyright © Therese Elgquist, 2020
Originally published in Sweden by The Book Affair, TBA Publishing AB
Published in 2021 under license from The Book Affair, TBA Publishing AB.

Skyhorse Publishing books may be purchased in bulk at special discounts
for sales promotion, corporate gifts, fund-raising, or educational purposes.
Special editions can also be created to specifications. For details, contact
the Special Sales Department, Skyhorse Publishing, 307 West 36th Street,
11th Floor, New York, NY 10018 or info@skyhorsepublishing.com.

Skyhorse® and Skyhorse Publishing® are registered trademarks of Skyhorse
Publishing, Inc.®, a Delaware corporation.

Visit our website at www.skyhorsepublishing.com.

10 9 8 7 6 5 4 3 2 1

Library of Congress Cataloging-in-Publication Data is available on file.

Cover design by David Ter-Avanesyan
Front cover photographs: cover by Shutterstock, plate by Therese Elgquist
Back cover photos (l-r) Therese Elgquist (2) and Agnes Maltesdotter

ISBN: 978-1-5107-6532-0
Ebook ISBN: 978-1-5107-6667-9

Printed in China

CONTENTS

WELCOME TO THE PLANT KINGDOM!

Your hands are holding a treasure, and not just any treasure. It is the key to perhaps the world's most contemporary cuisine. Exhilarating, delicious, and fabulously colorful food, full of flavors, textures, and nutrition. Welcome to a world where vegetables are cool, legumes are sexy, and food is scrumptious—a world of endless possibilities and great pleasures. Here is a place for everything: from baby food and weeknight dinners, to a fancy banquet!

Hop aboard an amazing food journey. You'll learn the foundations of a plant-based diet: how to build, create, flavor, and transform a multitude of dishes. You'll become a master at throwing together a spread from leftovers, preparing a full meal, or just blending some hummus. Effortlessly, you'll assemble vegetable tapas, toss an indulgent salad, whisk up delicious dressings, bake sourdough bread and lentil crackers, prepare tofu five different ways, and top a pizza with nut-based cheese.

Remember, "To be or not to be" is not the question here. *Plant-Based Cooking for Absolute Beginners* is an authentic way of talking about food, prepared exclusively from a variety of delicious ingredients from the plant kingdom. The plants are allowed to remain plants, served up without having to pretend they're something else. This is food offered without a lecture, food that is wholesome, and, yes, food that is frequently good for the environment, too.

Nobody needs to become vegan overnight (or ever) just because they add more plant-based meals to their diet; it is entirely up to each individual. Eating should not be a set of rules, nor is it an all-or-nothing endeavor. Eating a plant-based diet should bring you happiness—a joy from seed to plate. We partake in healthy diets and want to be emotionally moved by flavor.

This is my world, and I sincerely hope you will visit—and be able to create your own unique cuisine afterwards. Well, to be perfectly honest, I hope after browsing through this book's pages you'll be persuaded that vegetables are pretty cool, a snap to prepare, and very tasty.

Let's begin!

Thess

HOW TO NAVIGATE THE PLANT WORLD

Let's start with the basics. Here is the foundation, not just for a plant-based cuisine but for all kinds of cooking—tips, tricks, and tools that will make it all simpler, more accessible, sustainable, and fun to cook and eat really delicious food!

How to build an all-round basic pantry

You're off to a good start if you already have some staples. There are lots of possibilities when you have oils, vinegar, particular dry goods, pre-cooked legumes, spices, and other flavorings (I call them kitchen supports). Starting on page 28, you'll discover how to stock your pantry in a smart way in order to prepare everything in this book—and you'll get lots of other recipes, too.

Work smart—batch cook

Plan and prep! Bake two (2) sheets of root vegetables when you're at it. Cook a double batch of grains, make an extra large lentil stew, and mix a double batch of dips and dressings. The secret is starting with mostly the same ingredients and combining them differently for weekly meals using a well-stocked refrigerator filled with select produce. As a rule, plant-based ingredients keep several days in the refrigerator (and longer still in the freezer, for that matter) so you can prepare all food for the week in one go.

Vary more!

Select about four (4) or five (5) basic dishes to work with. These may have followed you all your life or you found some in this book. Vary them now and then by exchanging or adding a few new vegetables or other ingredients. Start out with one (1) and then with two (2) ingredients. Replace the stew's sweet potato with carrots; mix in some spinach with the pancake batter. When the urge hits, try a new dressing on a favorite salad; use toasted seeds instead of almonds. Make your favorite hummus using a different legume than you regularly use. Yellow peas, white beans, and red lentils are some of my hummus favorites, apart from the

1

classical chickpea version. Suddenly, you have many more recipes than the four (4) or five (5) you started out with. You can experiment a great deal if you always keep my ultimate formulas (they start on page 62) in the back of your mind. Don't forget to allow the season, in addition to what is in your refrigerator, help decide how to introduce variety in your dishes. Going beyond just varying entire dishes, it's easy to enhance individual ingredients in recipes. Play with, for example, infusing different flavors into grains. Add some ginger or lemon juice when you cook durra. Sprinkle a pinch of turmeric or splash in some coconut milk when you cook quinoa to give them exciting flavors.

"Makeovers" of leftovers

One of the greatest things we can do in the kitchen is transform leftovers into appetizing dishes. We might even say it is our superpower, because this saves nearly everything we care about: time, money, and environment. It means seeing the potential in yesterday's meal or fragments of an ingredient. A simple way to spiff up everything from brown bag lunches to yesterday's leftovers is to mix in a handful of leafy greens or fresh herbs to make the leftovers feel new again. Another suggestion is enhancing freshness by drizzling lemon juice and grating zest or adding a tart dressing on top. Check page 13 for how to give new life to vegetables and how to create, as if by magic, new dishes from leftovers.

Smart reverse cooking

Often perfectly fine foods end up in the garbage can. To rethink food shopping by checking the refrigerator, freezer, and pantry before heading out, is what I call smart reverse cooking. Quite simply, start at the opposite end. Using what you already have, work backwards instead of working on autopilot preparing your favorite dish with new ingredients. Concentrate on what you already have rather than on the preparation of a specific dish. Once you know what is readily available, you can use those ingredients to transform them into the dish you wanted to make. Reverse cooking is a great way to lessen food waste. Forgotten root vegetables at the back of the refrigerator, a cup or two of cooked grains, and a partial container of crushed tomatoes will guide your meal preparation. Stray leftovers that feel boring and useless on their own can be quite the opposite when you use them at the start. It is also often quicker to reverse cook, as half the meal or more may already be cooked.

Live seasonally

Eating seasonally as much as possible, ideally with locally grown produce, offers you better-tasting vegetables. They are often better value for your money as well. This practice is also good for the environment, considering vegetables grown and ripened naturally are more climate-friendly. They need less energy than those cultivated in heated energy-sucking greenhouses.

In some parts of the world we have distinct seasons—each of them producing their specific fruits and vegetables. This is something worth taking advantage of. We look upon it as a great opportunity when preparing our meals, as it becomes a natural way to vary our menus!

Start with one vegetable

Rethink, but in a new way! Get rid of the old classic mindset that certain meals are meant for certain weekdays. Try to build the menu around the current season's best-tasting and most price-wise produce. Then compose your meals from the produce you have chosen. Instead of thinking *today is soup day*, make a habit of thinking *carrots are in their prime just now, and luckily we have plenty of those in the refrigerator—what are we going to make with them? A soup would be good!* One way to get into the habit of thinking this way is to save recipes you like and index them by "main vegetables" instead by the type of dish (e.g. appetizer, entrée, dessert). This will make you more flexible and more food savvy in the kitchen. Read on page 50 how a single vegetable can take on many characteristics.

Don't go overboard with "trendy" vegetables

Sometimes certain vegetables or plants, for one reason or another, become trendy. Often, their perceived health-promoting properties get them the limelight. Truth be told, there are often other plants that have the same properties that aren't given fad status. Trendy plant produce (today's quinoa, açai, avocado, sweet potato, and coconut for example) is consumed in large quantities. It harms the environment when these plants are grown in huge quantities year after year (without beneficial crop rotation) to meet the demand. These plants often are grown in exotic locations and there's a need for long-distance transportation. Now, this doesn't mean that we necessarily have to stop eating all those things we like so much. However, we have to start contemplating how we can temper our consumption to reasonable levels. We need to look around us at all the great—and nutritious—produce we already have closer to home.

Start at your level

Start by learning how to prepare a really tasty hummus and how you can vary it. Spread it on your breakfast sandwich, add it to a salad, put it in a wrap, use it as the base for a hummus bowl, or dip vegetable sticks into it. Then add different hummus variations, more food knowledge, and new dishes each week—or at a speed comfortable for you. Before long, your repertoire has grown and plants have become a natural part of your food preparation. Look upon your food journey, regardless of your starting point, a bit like an endurance exercise. You don't start exercising by running a mile the first time out. Instead, you start with a reasonable distance, and increase this little by little as you get better at running. Who knows, you might soon be a marathon runner!

Trust your taste buds

We are talking about two (2) things here. First, we talk about cooking food you enjoy. Cooking is not an exact science. A bit more here or a bit less there of an ingredient doesn't always have an important impact. However, make a habit of taste-testing as you cook so you know if you need to adjust. A bit more salt, or perhaps more chili powder? Is the lentil stew a bit on the dry side? Should you leave the carrots in the oven a bit longer (after all, you do prefer them really soft)? Does the hummus need twice as much herb seasoning? Your taste buds will steer you!

You also need to trust your taste buds when you check if something is still edible. Is that plant-based yogurt way past its use-by date? Are those carrots too "tired" by now? Taste and you'll soon discover what is usable and what should be thrown out.

"PONDER" COOKIES WITH TAHINI AND CINNAMON

Well, we're on our way! But before we go any further I think we ought to have a first recipe. This is not just any recipe, but a recipe for Ponder Cookies. This is my name for the cookies I munch on when I arrive home really hungry, and I'm pondering what to prepare for dinner; or, perhaps, what I am munching on when reading a new thrilling book. The cookies are something between a sweet and a snack, with a crispy exterior and chewy interior.

Makes 12 cookies

Ingredients

2 cups rolled oats
½ tsp baking powder
1 tbsp cinnamon, ground
½ tsp cardamom, ground
½ tsp vanilla powder
1 pinch salt flakes
14 dates, fresh, pitted
½ cup light tahini
2 tbsp plant-based
    beverage or water
1 carrot, finely grated

How to: Preheat the oven to 350°F (175°C). In a food processor mix the first six ingredients and process into fine crumbs. Add the dates, and mix again to fine crumbs. Add the tahini and the liquid ingredients and pulse to form a dough. Add the grated carrot and pulse a few more times. Place 12 mounds of the mixture on a baking sheet and flatten them slightly. Bake the cookies about 15 to 17 minutes until they are slightly crisp with golden edges. Store the cookies in a jar with a tight-fitting lid, either in the refrigerator or freezer.

A GROWING (PLANT) WORLD

As you browse this book page by page you'll find a world full of potentials and you'll discover how the (plant) world grows in size for each new dish you put together and experience. The simple tips and tricks in the beginning of the book help you build a solid base to work from. A bit further along in the book we'll look closer at preparation and we'll dive into cooking guides and show loads of formulas and flowcharts pointing clearly to all the possibilities—and what results can be attained.

A CUISINE FULL OF POSSIBILITIES

Vegetables can be prepared in many different ways. Beets are made into burgers, or they are grated raw. Grate them into the porridge, or add them to bread dough or muffin batter, or dry them and mix them to a powder to sprinkle over a plant-based yogurt, a porridge, or a dessert. Beets can be made into hummus or be oven-baked whole, in pieces, or as thin chips, or any size in between. How a beet is prepared, i.e. the size, cut, and the cooking method, will all have an effect on its taste and texture. The same goes for most any vegetables you have seen.

The world contains more species of edible plants—and probably many more that we haven't discovered yet—than anybody could possibly try during their lifetime. This just refers to vegetables and legumes, grains, herbs, seeds, nuts, and other edibles. Imagine that you know ten (10) different vegetables among the enormous supply we have. Given the beets example, it is clear that each vegetable can be prepared at least 15 ways. That means you have 150 possible variations of prepared plant-based produce in your repertoire. Then imagine how many different ways you can serve these vegetables.

Further along in the book we'll dive more profoundly into preparation guides and a load of formulas and flowcharts that will show pretty clearly all the possibilities—and the results you can achieve by following them.

A DISH—SEVERAL WAYS

Here's a thought experiment. I will shortly give you six (6) raw ingredients. No, I won't send them to you, at your present location (wouldn't that be fun to have them flying in just at this moment); this is pure imagination. I want you to take paper and pen and write down what you would do if the six (6) ingredients were waiting on your kitchen counter when you arrive home, hungry, after a long day at work. You do have a few staples already—oil, toasted nuts, tahini, and frozen herbs—things that are good to always have on hand so your food prep is more flexible.

Quinoa
Carrots
Kale
Apple
Chickpeas, cooked
Plant-based yogurt

What would you have cooked? Once you've written it down, take a look at page 122 where you'll find three different dishes that I made from just the ingredients provided.

There is a lesson here. That 1) there are a myriad of ways to prepare plant-based ingredients and create different dishes. 2) It is OK to experiment in the kitchen! Hand on heart, I promise you that the dishes I've written about on page 122 are scrumptious! Just as I know that yours will be, too!

SEASONAL PRODUCE GUIDE

"Eat seasonally" are buzzwords all over the food world today. In spite of this, our grocery stores are mostly filled with the same kind of produce all year round, which makes it difficult to understand what is actually in season.

You can buy staples like grains, nuts, seeds, and different spices and flavorings, and frozen produce whenever you wish; they are not dependent on seasons in the same way that fresh produce is.

Harvest months for produce may vary somewhat from year to year. Produce availability depends on, among other things, weather conditions, harvest quantity, and cultivation methods (outside or in greenhouses). Make it a habit to check labels on all fresh produce to learn the provenance of the produce. Some plants like root vegetables and onions are available year round because, when stored properly, they keep longer.

Credit: Agnes Maltesdotter

KITCHEN HACKS

Less waste—more money in your wallet

Do you dream about reducing food waste and getting as much great food as possible for your money? There are probably many having the same dream. How do we go about realizing it? I suggest we dig up a bunch of great tips and tricks again!

A commonly held misconception is that eating a nutritious plant-based diet is expensive and that you'll need a lot of weird and expensive ingredients. Nothing is further from the truth. Those "special" ingredients are very seldom an important part of preparing appetizing, green, and nutritious food. In fact, we manage extremely well on locally sourced ingredients and by using simple staples that are generally inexpensive. Using spices and seasonings (among other flavorings), and chiefly by how we combine them in dishes, enables us to transform "commonplace ingredients" into something both exciting and delectable.

Here you'll get some of my best tips for reducing food waste and also how to save on expense. You'll soon see how these two things go together, without having to compromise on either flavor or nutrition.

ECO (SMART) TIPS

Waste less

Get your housekeeping money to go further by not wasting food. It comes down to drawing on your resources more effectively by making use of spoonfuls of leftovers and those half-forgotten vegetables at the bottom of the refrigerator. Simple things that make the budget stretch further. This is basic math. A third of the world's food production ends up as waste, which is basically throwing money in the trash.

Eat seasonal produce

You've seen this several times already but it bears repeating: save money by buying and eating seasonal produce!

Freeze produce when the prices are lowest

Take the opportunity to buy—or pick—seasonal produce when it is offered at sale prices and then freeze what you are not using immediately.

Maybe you even have free produce in nature. Collect it yourself and profit from the fresh air and exercise. Perhaps take a quiet pause in the woods with a cup of hot chocolate, among mushrooms or blueberry bushes.

Cook your own legumes and make your own plant milks

Most grocery stores sell pre-cooked legumes in aseptic packaging for a relatively reasonable price. It saves a lot of money if you soak and cook them yourself, and it is not difficult at all! Just make sure to soak the legumes overnight in plenty of water, and then cook them the next day. Do big-batch cooking and freeze in smaller packs so as to have for plenty of future meals. This way each portion will only cost pennies—all depending on the ingredients, of course. You can save even more money by making your own plant-based beverages—see how to on page 21.

Plan your shopping and stay realistic

Planning your shopping trip increases the chance you will actually use what you've spent your hard-earned cash on. A "3-for-2" offer is pretty meaningless if you only have time to use up a ⅓ of the produce.

WASTE (NOT) TIPS

Don't forget the exterior

Most vegetables (even root vegetables) are more flavorful and get a more distinct texture if the peel is left on when cooked. In addition, the peel usually contains a great deal of nutrients, so it becomes a win-win situation. If you still want to peel certain produce, like root vegetables, because the peel is very thick, save the peel. Mix it into a smoothie or a soup, where you're not bothered by the peel's taste or texture, but you still get the nutritional benefit. Another fun thing to try is making peel chips. Brush the peel with some oil and sprinkle over a pinch of salt. Place the peel on a baking sheet and roast in a 305°F (150°C) oven for about 10 to 15 minutes or until the peel is golden and crisp. Scrumptious both for snacking or a topping for most everything.

Herbs + oil = reinvigorate

When herbs start to look a bit droopy and tired, mix them to a paste with some cold-pressed good-quality oil and freeze in individual ice tray cubes. The cubes are perfect for blending into dips, dressings, soups, or vegetable burger mix.

Dry bread

Freshly baked bread is unbeatable with some good quality oil or flavorful cold cuts. However, once a loaf has dried up and turned a bit too tough, we don't have to leave it to its fate, because we can find other uses for it. Steam it a few seconds to liven it up. Toast whole slices, make croutons, or prepare bread and cabbage crumbs (the recipe is further down on the page)—those are just a few suggestions to consider.

Leftover shelf

Organize the refrigerator! Select a shelf and designate it the place where you collect all the leftovers. Keep, perhaps, a container with vegetables that need to be used up sooner rather than later, in order to not forget anything. This is a very simple and effective way to have a check on what you already have on hand and to lessen food waste.

REDUCE WASTE
Discover new usage for produce that often ends up in the garbage can. Day-old bread and cabbage stems—the latter is often left over in my kitchen—are made into a great topping! Never mind if you don't have the exact quantities of bread and cabbage in the recipe; just adjust the amount of oil to your number of ingredients. Only a little oil is needed.

BREAD AND CABBAGE CRUMBS
<u>Ingredients</u>
2 slices day-old sourdough bread
2 handfuls stems from Tuscan cabbage and kale
1 small garlic clove
½ tsp French tarragon, dried
1 tbsp olive oil
1 pinch salt flakes

How to: Preheat the oven to 305°F (150°C). In a food processor, chop sourdough bread and stems into small crumbs. Add finely grated garlic, dried tarragon, olive oil, and salt flakes, then pulse several times. Spread the crumbs on a baking sheet and roast for about 45 minutes until everything is dry and crisp. Store the crumbs in an airtight container.

From discards to festive

Here's some solid tips on how to use your superpowers to create a party out of leftovers, and also how to adopt the mindset you'll need to be able to make it a habit.

- Leftover roasted root vegetables can be mixed into a soup or flavor a hummus.
- Do you have a spoonful of leftover cooked quinoa or some other grain? Mix it with chopped vegetables and use it as topping for a soup (or a sandwich) to add mouth-feel, or stir it into the oat porridge.
- Remember what you did with your leftovers. Make a base of creamy hummus in a bowl from grilled asparagus, leftover potato salad, and a small handful of nuts. Other smart dishes you can prepare with leftovers might be some pizza, a wrap, or a filling porridge that can be topped with different kinds of leftovers.
- If you're batch cooking, make a habit of roasting, for example, plain root vegetables. This means you can eat some root vegetables any day, each time seasoned differently or mixed with different dressings to get some variation. Do the same when you marinate or cook legumes or grains.

Correct storage

Using a refrigerator correctly makes a big difference in the food's shelf life. Always keep the refrigerator at 39 to 40°F (4°C). Make sure that packaging is closed properly. Store cooked foods in lidded containers to avoid it getting dry and stale, or spoiling. Avoid storing raw produce too close together. Vegetables need breathing space to stay fresh. Certain vegetables and fruits like tomatoes, cucumber, avocado, banana, and citrus fruits are better stored outside the refrigerator.

KITCHEN CHAMPIONS

Basic activities like planning and preparing are necessary to simplify everyday cooking so you end up with delicious meals. A few small simple tricks will help you along, so you can enjoy all meals throughout the day without having to resort to time-consuming preparation each day. You'll need some help to achieve this—and not just any help.

Below is a collection of my "kitchen champions" (soon to be yours, too). They are just what they sound like: basic ingredients that stock a pantry, refrigerator, and freezer, enabling you to simplify, beautify, and vary your cooking. Last but not least, this cooking is kind to your pocketbook and the environment. A well-provisioned kitchen will usually have grains, precooked legumes, seeds and nuts, spice mixes, frozen vegetables and berries, tasty bread or rye crackers, different flavorings, and cold-pressed oils. A newly toasted granola might also be waiting on the kitchen counter as well as some homemade spice mixes—but we'll return to those later. Use your kitchen champions, i.e. your basic staples, combined with existing stocked green produce, then go ahead and add seasonal fresh vegetable and fruits.

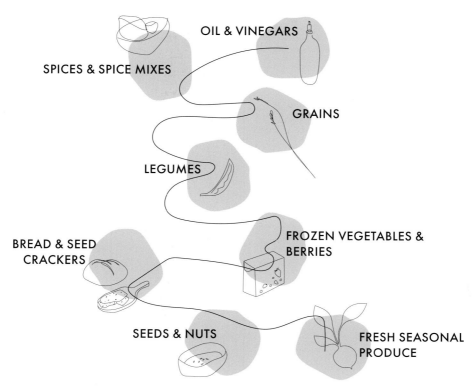

OIL & VINEGARS

SPICES & SPICE MIXES

GRAINS

LEGUMES

BREAD & SEED CRACKERS

FROZEN VEGETABLES & BERRIES

SEEDS & NUTS

FRESH SEASONAL PRODUCE

PANTRY CHAMPIONS

With these ingredients in the pantry, your cooking will be like child's play. Several of the ingredients can be store-bought; examples are the spice mixes, rye crackers, and granola. Now, if you want to, it is just as easy to make them yourself (because it is both great fun and it saves money).

Grains

Grains are sold whole, crushed, flaked, as groats, and ground into flour. Each style serves a different function.

There are many different grains with long shelf-life in the pantry. When cooked, they are perfect as a base for salads or stews, as fillers for burgers, or as toppings for soup. Spelt; quinoa; naked oats [*Avena nuda, Avena chinensis*]; barley; groats; sorghum; durra; wild, red, black, and brown rice; and amaranth are just some for you to choose from. Cook them separately or, if some have the same prep time, cook them together for more interest.

Then there are grains like crushed oats, flattened oats like rolled oats, sorghum, or spelt flakes. Crushed grains and flakes are handy to have at home both for making a quick porridge, soaking an overnight porridge in the refrigerator, or to use for baking. Add some rolled oats to the dough batter for more moist scones!

If you keep a selection of different flours in your pantry, throwing together a pancake batter, baking bread or buns, or making waffles can be done in no time at all. In other words, nothing we want to miss out on! I usually keep spelt flour at home and use it to bake sourdough bread. I also keep oat flour and buckwheat flour for other baked goods or for pancakes.

Spice mixes and salt mixes

Seasonings can lift a dish to new heights, especially if you used multi-spice mixtures. Spice mixtures are a good option if you have limited shelf space. Make a habit of keeping something spicier for soups and stews, as well as something herby for grilled summer vegetables or yogurt sauces. A mild but spicy seasoning is good for falafel or baked root vegetables. For porridge and morning drinks, preferably something warming: a golden, somewhat sweet mix of cinnamon, ginger, turmeric, and cardamom. Apart from spice mixes I always have salt flakes, whole peppercorns in the grinder, cinnamon, turmeric, paprika powder, cumin, coriander, and fennel seeds.

Salt mixes are similar to spice mixes but with characteristics of their own. Salt flakes are mixed with different spices, and perhaps some nuts and seeds, to make a salt mix. They are tasty "all-in-one" toppings suitable for many dishes from breakfast porridge to holiday desserts. The recipes on pages 100 and 101 show you how to make your own spice and salt mixes!

Granola

Granola is a favorite topping for plant-based yogurt, chia pudding, and porridge. You can vary a granola with lots of different kinds of seeds, nuts, groats, and crushed grains. You can also add dried fruits, berries, and coconut flakes. Each granola can be different if you flavor with different spices like cinnamon, cardamom, turmeric, and allspice. To create a sweeter granola, mix water, oil, and a few fresh dates. Then stir in the dry ingredients. If you leave out the spices and dates the granola will taste more savory and is perfectly suited for topping on salads! After all this talk about granola, here is a simple basic recipe!

GRANOLA, BASIC RECIPE

This will make about 2 ½ cups

<u>Ingredients</u>
2 cups grains
2 cups mixed seeds/nuts
approx. 1 tbsp spices (a mixture of cinnamon, ginger, turmeric, cardamom, allspice)
1 large pinch salt flakes
1 cup finely grated carrot or parsnip—your choice
½ cup water
2 tbsp oil
2 fresh dates, pitted (for a sweet granola)
1 handful dried berries/fruit (raisins, goji berries, mulberries, apricots, berries, apple)
1 handful coconut chips or ½ handful cacao nibs

How to: Preheat the oven to 350°F (175°C), or 305°F (150°C) if you're using a convection oven and roasting both sheets at once. Mix the first four ingredients and add the grated root vegetable. Heat the water and oil and, if making a sweet granola, mix in the fresh dates. Stir in the grain mixture. Spread the mixture over two baking sheets. Toast in the oven about 45 minutes or until the granola is crunchy. Add dried fruit or berries and perhaps some coconut chips or cacao nibs. Store the granola in a jar on a kitchen shelf—it has nearly unlimited shelf life!

Seed crackers

A really crisp cracker adds appetizing texture and flavor. It goes great with a tofu scramble at breakfast, or with a soup if topped with a creamy hummus and sprouts. For that relaxed Friday family evening, why not try it as a snack with a yummy dip? In other words, a cracker is always handy! P.S.: Crumbled crackers can also serve as topping in a pinch!

Precooked legumes

Fortunately, there are loads of different kinds of precooked canned beans and lentils available in the grocery stores. These are practical if you don't want, or don't have time, to soak and cook legumes yourself. Black beans are perfect for plant-based burgers. Different kinds of white beans can be blended for dips or fillers for soups; add them to scones dough, or marinate them and serve as a side dish. Chickpeas make a great base for falafel, burgers, hummus, and other dips. Simply rinse and puree them for a simple dressing. Marinade them for a tasty side to go with most dishes, or use as a filling addition to a salad. You'll find plenty of suggestions—even a surprise sweet—for what to do with just chickpeas, on page 116!

Oils

A good-quality cold-pressed oil has its place in the kitchen. Drizzle oil over a salad before serving or stir it into a bean dip for extra delicious flavor, creaminess, and nutrition. Depending on what flavor I'm after I always keep, at the minimum, cold-pressed canola oil and cold-pressed olive oil for variety. These oils are good on their own, but I also use them for dressings, sauces, and marinades. Apart from the delicious natural oils, there are also plenty of flavored oils: garlic, lemon, herb, and even truffle oil. It's a handy shortcut to adding flavors to different ingredients. Go ahead and marinade cooked beans in oil, or massage thinly shredded raw cabbage with oil until the cabbage is softened. Warm-pressed canola oil is best for frying, as it has a higher smoking point.

Vinegar

Vinegar is a must in the kitchen. It rounds off the taste in soups, stews, dips, marinades, and dressings like nothing else. Vinegar makes it a breeze to quickly pickle vegetables. There are plenty of different vinegars out there but, if you're only going for one, choose an apple cider vinegar that suits all occasions. It adds a nice tart tinge with a slightly sweet note.

Tamari soy sauce

Tamari is a gluten-free soy sauce. It imparts a deeper, but less salty taste than the common soy sauce. Make sure you always have some tamari (or a soy sauce that you like) on hand to add to marinades, sauces, and dressings.

Nutritional yeast

Brewer's yeast is also a kind of nutritional yeast but imparts a bitter flavor.[*] Both are obvious members of the plant-based kitchen champions. Nutritional yeast imparts an appetizing cheese flavor and a slight nuttiness, making it a perfect addition to bean dips or kale chips (which you massage with oil, nutritional yeast, and salt before baking them in the oven). Add a few teaspoons of nutritional yeast to dressings for a more intense flavor. Sprinkle some between the layers in lasagna. Add it to nut cheese (see recipes on page 109). A little nutritional yeast is good wherever you need cheese flavor. Nutritional yeast is sold in well-stocked grocery stores, health food stores, and online.

Nutritional yeast is never a brewery by-product, and is typically grown on molasses from either sugar beets or cane sugar. Much of the sugar beet harvest in the US is genetically modified, but nutritional yeasts grown on non-GMO versions are available, and some are organic.

Psyllium husk and chia seeds

Powdered psyllium seed husk is incredibly fiber-rich and contains a great capacity to absorb water to form a sort of gel. This gel is very useful to bind dough when baking gluten-free breads or seed crackers. A pinch of this powder will also thicken a sauce. Start with a knife's edge because psyllium husk powder expands enormously when mixed with a liquid.
Chia seeds have similar characteristics and can also be used to bind ingredients when baking gluten-free goods. Mix chia seeds in a smoothie for creaminess. Soak chia seeds overnight for a morning porridge (see recipe on page 91). Also, use them for making a berry jam: mix 7 oz mashed berries with 2 teaspoons chia seeds and let the mixture swell to form jam.

Raw nuts, almonds, and seeds

Nuts, almonds, and seeds are perfect for toppings; making granola; eating as snacks; and using in baking. Soak raw nuts and seeds overnight and then toast them in a 170°F (75°C) oven until they are dry and crisp. This way the nuts are easier to digest, and their deliciously flavorful nutrition is more easily absorbed! Roast raw nuts and seeds. Mix them with some salt and chili powder, turmeric, or the salt and turmeric spice mix from page 101 for a change. These are perfect snacks to take on the go or to have as toppings for dishes. I store raw nuts and seeds in the refrigerator for the longest shelf life. Roasted nuts and seeds meant for quick consumption can be kept at room temperature. It's nice to have nut flours around, too, for baking. Almond flour is my favorite!

---

*https://www.betternutrition.com/supplements/brewers-yeast-versus-nutritional-yeast/: Brewer's yeast is traditionally a by-product of the beer-making process, in which case it's cultivated on malted barley or other grains, which produces some bitterness. However, some brewer's yeasts are "primary grown," meaning they are cultivated specifically for use as a dietary supplement, and may be grown on the same types of media as nutritional yeast.

REFRIGERATOR CHAMPIONS

I divide my refrigerator champions into basic ingredients and prepared items. The basic ingredients are essentially flavor enhancers or store-bought items. The prepared items are finished or part of finished dishes. You'll soon discover that the latter often build on components you've read about earlier in the text, among the pantry champions, and later on, among the freezer champions.

Nut, almond, and seed butters

With nut or seed butter in your home, it's easy to mix an extremely silky smooth dressing. Need a recipe? Mix equal parts seed or nut butter with water and a splash of vinegar or freshly squeezed citrus. Add salt to taste. Then maybe add a flavoring like ginger, chili, tamari/soy sauce, lemon, or turmeric. I store nut and seed butters in the refrigerator for longer shelf life. If you're not planning to keep them over an extended period you may store them in the pantry.

Plant-based yogurt and oat, almond, soy, and coconut milk

To avoid unnecessary sweeteners, choose a plain plant-based yogurt and add berries as flavoring. The plain variety will work for both sweet and savory concoctions. Throw together appetizing sauces, use the yogurt in baking, or use it to top soups.

You can purchase plant-based beverages or make your own. Soak 1 part almonds/oats/pumpkin seeds in 4 parts water overnight. The next day, mix this in a blender until you have a smooth liquid. Strain the liquid through a cheesecloth or nut milk bag. It will keep for 3 to 4 days if refrigerated. Save any leftover pulp and add it to the next batch of falafel or vegetable burgers—bye, bye food waste and welcome delicious falafel!

Tofu and tempeh

Tofu is a highly protein-rich food product made from soybeans. It is sold as firm, smoked, or silken; it's found in the vegan section with the refrigerated foods. Different kinds of tofu have different uses. Firm tofu is wonderful when marinated and breaded or fried plain until lightly golden. Mix a good dressing to accompany the tofu or make a filling tofu scramble. Smoked tofu can be used as is, cubed into a salad, or thinly sliced for sandwich fixings. Silken tofu is excellent for sauces, desserts, and custards in pies and tarts. Be sure to choose organic tofu products. European Union–produced tofu protects you from the high levels of pesticides that are commonly found in tofu from other countries. Tempeh is another soy product that also can be found among refrigerated food items. In tempeh, the soybeans are fermented. Today you'll find tempeh in most well stocked grocery stores, and you'll also find tempeh made from a large variety of other legumes, for example, green and yellow peas. Try various tempeh products until you find one you prefer, as flavors vary with manufacturers. Tempeh has a clear distinct taste. There are milder versions, which I prefer. Marinated and fried tempeh can be eaten in a salad, used plain as ground meat substitute, or cubed for soup. You'll find tempeh recipes on page 119.

Mustard

It takes no time at all to mix together a vegan mayonnaise when you have a jar of mustard in the kitchen. The same goes for plenty of other dressings, too! Dijon mustard is the one to use for mayonnaise; for other dressings use Dijon or Skåne. [*]

Sauerkraut

A few spoonfuls of sauerkraut add a fantastic tart edge and freshness to salads, wraps, vegetable burgers, and other enticing dishes. Sauerkraut is also loaded with beneficial bacteria for a healthy gut flora. You can make your own sauerkraut, although it's available in the refrigerated section in most grocery stores.

Miso

Miso paste, with its incredible umami flavor, is made from fermented soybeans. What on earth is umami? Hurry to page 40 to get super knowledgeable! Miso is great mixed with some oil and then brushed onto baked root vegetables. The paste comes in a light and a dark version. The dark version has been fermented longer and has a stronger umami flavor. Depending on whether you use the light or dark version, you have to taste test to see how much to use in a recipe. Miso is sold in well-stocked grocery stores and also in shops specializing in organic products.

Seasonal vegetables

Once you have your staples, your green base, it is time to add fresh seasonal produce!

---

*https://www.tasteatlas.com/skansk-senap

Prepared items

The refrigerator is, as I've already mentioned, the perfect place for storing prepared ingredients for future meals. I store everything in individual glass jars so I can quickly and simply put together combinations of a dish, varying and including different items. That way, I arrive at many different dishes, but all starting from the same base!

- Some kind of hummus or other dip
- 1–2 dressings—alternative is a seed or nut butter
- 1–2 kinds of cooked grains and legumes—or the latter precooked, store-bought packaged
- Baked root vegetables or other vegetables, depending on seasonal availability
- Some form of falafel, vegetable burgers, marinated tempeh, or tofu. If I batch cooked falafel and burgers you will even find some in the freezer.

PLANT SHOT

Ready for another refrigerator champion? A bottle of homemade super shots—super because they are super delicious and they will (figuratively) kick-start any morning. All honors go to my mom for this recipe!

MOM'S TURMERIC AND GINGER SHOT

Makes a 25½ oz (750 ml) bottle

Ingredients
2 organic lemons
2 organic oranges
2 carrots—optional
1¾ oz fresh organic turmeric root
7 oz fresh organic ginger root
2½ cups water
⅕ tsp freshly ground black pepper

How to: Peel the citrus fruits—preferably grate the zest first and save for use in cooking or baking! Rinse the carrots, turmeric, and ginger. Cut citrus and carrots into smaller pieces and put it all through a slow juicer. Mix the juice with water and black pepper. This juice will keep refrigerated for up to 7 days. Shake thoroughly before drinking. If you don't own a slow juicer, grate the turmeric and ginger and leave to soak in the water for an hour or two. Strain the liquid and mix with freshly squeezed citrus and ground black pepper.

FREEZER CHAMPIONS

Go ahead and stock the freezer with frozen herbs, vegetables, and berries that are difficult to find fresh. Also stock with soup and smoothie vegetables that are going to be blended. Leftovers, batches of vegetarian burgers, and brown-bag items also earn a space in the freezer.

Soup vegetables

I like to make soups from vegetables like pumpkin, squash, cauliflower, spinach, green peas, and carrots. Several of these vegetables can be purchased frozen. The frozen equivalent is absolutely acceptable if what I want to use is not in season. Green peas, cauliflower, and spinach are also perfect to add to smoothies or smoothie bowls. Do you have some fresh vegetables stragglers left behind? Cube them, steam a few minutes, then cool and freeze. Voilà! You have your "bespoke" soup fixings in the freezer.

Berries

The season for berries is short in Sweden, but the berries live in the freezer section all year round. Take a look there if you want some out-of-season berries. The fresh berries we find in our grocery stores during the off-season months have to be flown in from other countries, often far away. This hardly makes them environmentally friendly.

Frozen fresh herbs

Dried herbs taste slightly different from their fresh relatives. However, they taste nearly the same when frozen as when they are fresh. If you're not planning to use them for decorating a dish, frozen herbs work just as well as fresh ones. You can flavor most dishes like dips, mashable veggies, marinades, stews, soups, dressings, burgers, or falafel with herbs.

Sourdough bread or rye bread

Nothing beats getting a slice of good bread from the freezer. A short moment in the oven and it tastes nearly freshly baked. Buy or bake your own bread and freeze it sliced. My best spelt sourdough bread is on page 107.

SHOPPING LIST

Perhaps you already have several of these ingredients in your kitchen, or do they feel totally foreign to you? Here's a shopping list to help you along. Why not bring the whole book or a photocopied list along on the next shopping trip?

Because they last longer, pantry and freezer staples are not something you need to shop for each week. The objective of staples is always having some at home. You just need to remember to add fresh produce in order to throw together really nice dishes.

PANTRY
Cold-pressed canola oil—for flavor
Warm-pressed canola oil—for frying
Cold-pressed olive oil—for flavor
Salt, flakes and fine grain
Whole black pepper for grinding. Freshly ground pepper tastes best!
Apple cider vinegar

2–3 different whole grains
For example quinoa, whole oats with bran, sorghum (millet), buckwheat; wild, brown, red, and black rice

1–2 grains
For example sorghum, oats, quinoa, spelt, rye

1–2 different flours
For example oat, buckwheat, chickpea, spelt, and almond flour

3–4 spice mixes
Store-bought or make your own. See recipes on pages 100 to 101.

1–2 nuts or almonds
Cashews, almonds, walnuts, Brazil nuts, hazelnuts, macadamia nuts. They're all great for raw food pastries, müsli, and as toppings for dishes. Cashews or blanched almonds work best for nut cheese.

1–2 seeds
Pumpkin and sunflower seeds, chia seeds, flax seeds, hemp seeds (hearts), camelina (false flax) seeds

Nutritional yeast
Brewer's yeast
Tamari/soy sauce
Psyllium husk

FRUITS AND VEGETABLES

6–8 seasonal vegetables

Buy these in-season. See suggestion below and mix to get a selection of vegetables. Don't feel frightened because it looks like a lot. We include basic staple vegetables, too, in this list.

1–2 root vegetable or pumpkin
Parsnip, carrots, celeriac, beets, butternut squash, Hokkaido squash, Muscat squash. These have long shelf lives and keep for at least several weeks in the refrigerator.

1–2 cabbages
Tuscan cabbage, kale, green cabbage, pointed cabbage, fennel, Brussels sprouts

1–2 leafy greens
Spinach, mâche, mixed lettuce leaf, arugula

1–2 assorted vegetables
Cucumber, tomatoes, zucchini, bell peppers, eggplant, beans, mushrooms. Onions and garlic. The last ones function as bases for a lot of dishes, so make sure that you always have them at home!

FREEZER STAPLES

Herbs

Leafy greens
Spinach, kale for smoothies, stews, and soups

Cauliflower
For smoothies, soups, mash, raw-food ice-cream

Green peas
For smoothies, soups, burgers, and dips

Peas and beans
Haricots verts green beans, garden peas, garden beans

Berries
Sourdough bread

REFRIGERATOR STAPLES

Tofu
Firm and smoked, also silken if you want to make a pie

Tempeh

Plant-based yogurt—plain

Sauerkraut

Miso

Mustard

THE ULTIMATE OUTFITTED PANTRY

HOW TO BUILD A DISH

There are mathematical formulas, physics' basic laws, chemistry's periodic table, music's notational scales, printing's ABC's . . . and then there is food theory!

Once you have grasped the principles for how to cook appetizing plant-based food we'll proceed to the next step: recipes 2.0. The formulas and flowcharts on the following pages will hopefully open up and simplify your food world. These pages will make you see connections you'd never imagined but your tongue and palate have always known. The information will make you understand how certain flavors and textures fit together with each other and why your favorite dishes have become just that, favorites. Believe me, this didn't happen by coincidence.

Perhaps the idea of formulas in connection with food sounds complicated to you. You will see it's not complicated at all. Thinking about it, a traditional recipe is in fact a formula. Look at it this way: the ingredient list is the information fed into the formula; the preparation—the how-to—is the formula itself; the completed dish is the answer/result. In fact, every time you've cooked you've used formulas without being conscious of it. The difference here is that I have broken down the formulas. You will learn, once and for all, how to take on the task (e.g. how to get tasty, nutritious, and varied food onto the table) in a somewhat new way.

Let's do a mental exercise before we continue. Imagine that you're in math class asking the teacher to help you with a problem. You're wondering about the right way to approach a problem in order to solve it. Instead of explaining how to structure the solution, in other words how to arrive at the solution, the teacher tells you to look in the back of the book. That's where the answer is printed. Problem solved.

Isn't this similar to how we work when cooking? Following a recipe down to the last letter instead of trying to understand the food composition and the thinking behind the construction? We may read, follow, and prepare all the recipes in the world—however, not until we learn the construction behind a dish does a whole new world open up to us. You can then, confidently, put your own touch on the recipes in many different ways—both old and tried, and new ones. Two recipes suddenly turn into ten because you substituted and added three new vegetables, depending on what you have on hand and what your craving tells you to add. For example, when you use sorghum instead of quinoa because it's left over from yesterday's dinner; or try a new dressing on a favorite burger; or flavor the hummus with yesterday's roasted parsnip. Even though the stew was missing a 1/2 cup crushed tomatoes, the dinner still arrived on the table.

When you *understand* the formulas and construction that goes into food preparation you will not only be introduced to a whole new world of possibilities, you will also see your world in an entirely different way.

Before we grab the book and leap into the kitchen to try the dishes, let's take a quick tour around taste, textures, and nutrition—the very essence of all food.

TASTE, TEXTURE, AND NUTRITION

Taste, texture, and nutrition is the secret behind really delicious food—food that is exciting and fills you up, wherein every mouthful is an experience. Together the three elements comprise the whole we need to make everything from midweek breakfast to the most festive dinner of the year. We'll take a closer look at specific building blocks within each element to grasp the different tastes, textures, and nutritional groups we have to play with . . . because we are going to *play* with our food!

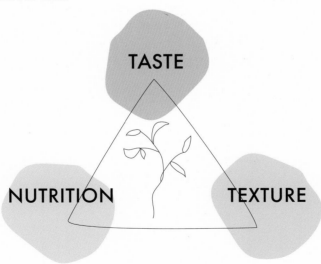

THE CHEMISTRY OF TASTE AND TEXTURE

Sweet, sour, salt, bitter, and umami are our five basic tastes. We are able to detect many aromas and experience more flavors because of a cooperation between our nose and mouth. Early on, it was probably our ability to detect these basic tastes that helped us select what to eat or what to avoid because it might harm us. Sweet and fatty ingredients were good because they provided much-needed calories and nourishment. A sour taste could indicate that something was too old. The item might even have been poisonous if it tasted bitter. This explains why we are partial to sweet and fatty foods, and why some (especially children) shy away from sour and bitter tastes.

Tastes That Marry Well

Did you think it was just a coincidence that sour lemon custard goes extremely well with a sweet piecrust? That the taste of a tart tomato soup is enhanced by a bit of added sweetness? That mushrooms and onions give a fall stew (and many other dishes) a certain appetizing depth? Is it by pure chance that you favor certain foods, or that some classical dishes have stood the test of time? There is nothing strange about this at all. In all probability these dishes have a certain balance between basic tastes and many different textures. I'll show you an example by offering the recipe for one of my absolute favorite snacks. I absolutely adore tahini-stuffed fresh dates with cacao, cranberry powder, and salt. I call them "Chemistry of Taste Dates."

TIP COLUMN
·
Chemistry of Taste Dates

Pit a fresh date and stuff the date with a small spoonful of your yummiest nut, almond, or seed butter. Dust with cacao and perhaps some cranberry powder. Finally, sprinkle with some salt flakes. Yours to relish!

The recipe combines all the elements: sweetness from the date, saltiness from the salt flakes, sourness from the cranberry powder, and bitterness from the cacao powder. It also has different textures (which we will examine shortly) from the date's creaminess, the tahini's smoothness, and the crispness of the salt flakes. Fat, when combined with other ingredients, is superb at enhancing the tastes. Here we get fat from the tahini. It is therefore perfectly normal that my brain performs somersaults when it discovers that I'm eating tahini-stuffed dates.

Fatty goodness

Fat is an important part of the food we eat; not just because of its nutritional value, but also because it adds to our taste experience and appreciation of the dish as a whole, i.e. mouthfeel. I'm sure most of us have a favorite dish or two that includes fat. Fat is often described as a flavor carrier because, thanks to its aromatic compounds, different flavors that marry well with fat are accentuated. Plant-based foods usually contain less fat than traditional dishes, so it doesn't hurt for us to add fat in the form of specific plant ingredients that contain plenty of fat. Think of nuts and seeds, avocado, kale or root vegetable chips, deep-fried onions, and dressings made from nut butter or cold-pressed oils. So, it is both delicious and nutritious to add some healthy fats to each meal.

Temperature

Food's palatability is also affected by temperature. Warm food usually has more flavors. For example, a spicy chili stew gives a tamer impression if eaten cold. A simple rule of thumb is that the more varied temperatures within a dish, the more exciting each mouthful will be. If you follow my instructions on how to build texture you will automatically arrive at different temperatures: baked slightly warm vegetables mixed with room-temperature raw crisp vegetables. The whole meal might be served with a cool yogurt sauce.

COMPLETE TASTE

A dollop of a tart cream on top of a sweet dessert will make it even more delectable. Umami gives the stew fuller depth, and a pinch of salt will enhance the flavors in all dishes.

SWEET   SOUR   SALT   BITTER   UMAMI

The basic tastes in cooking are similar to any building's framing structure. By including all the above sensations (or at least as many as possible), taste-wise, you'll end up with a dish that feels complete.

In the taste school below we'll look closer at the different basic flavors and where we can find them in the plant kingdom. Before long, you'll easily determine how to use them so a stew's tastes, or a salad or cake's flavors "marry," as the saying goes.

SWEET

Sweetness doesn't just belong in desserts. Savory dishes can also benefit from a touch of sweetness. An addition of sweetness to savory foods nicely enhances the rest of the flavors. So what do we mean by sweetness? Are we talking about pure table sugar? Sometimes. However, there are plenty of ingredients from the plant kingdom that are naturally sweet. There is a reason why they have names like "sugar snap peas" and "sweet potatoes." Dried and fresh fruits add fine sweetness to everything from salads (thinly slice apples for the winter salad or put plum wedges in the summer one) to stews (a few chopped apricots or raisins in the lentil stew work wonders) and dips. Plant-based beverages like oat and coconut milk have a certain inherent sweetness, too.

These raw ingredients are naturally very sweet: Dried fruit, fresh fruit, fresh green peas, squash, sweet potatoes [yams], parsnip, corn, grilled bell pepper, fried onion, coconut milk, and oat milk.

SOUR

A sour addition rounds out any dish or dip and counteracts sweetness in an appetizing way. Try adding a splash of apple cider vinegar to the soup when done—the effect is nearly magical. Sweet, sun-ripe strawberries marinated in lime and mint reach new heights in terms of taste. Sourness is usually associated with freshness and refreshing tastes, and it works well to lighten up heavier dishes. Sourness expertly perks up those leftovers in the refrigerator.

These raw ingredients are naturally very sour: citrus fruits, vinegar, apples, rhubarb, and pickled or fermented vegetables.

SALT

This one is almost too simple. I'm sure many times you've experienced how salt enhances tastes and dishes. Tread easy at first, because just as a pinch of salt can heighten the taste experience, one too much can also sink a dish like a stone and make it unpalatable. Make sure to have a good salt in the kitchen (yes, there is a difference between salts) and use it to taste. Common table salt (often used in the food industry) is highly refined, i.e. treated, so the salt ends up mostly sodium chloride combined with a non-caking element. Sodium chloride is something we should avoid as much as possible. Table salt is tarter, and the taste often overwhelms other flavors. Mineral, mountain, and sea salts contain important minerals that we need. It's imperative, not only for flavor but from a nutritional standpoint, to choose the right kind of salt.

These raw ingredients are naturally very salty: salt and tamari/soy sauce.

BITTER

Most of us don't frequently associate bitterness as a sensation with pleasant food memories. Of course, there isn't really anything tempting about a raw kale leaf, a single arugula leaf, or a dessert with just a bit too much cacao powder. Now think how appetizing kale massaged with oil and salt is, or arugula mixed with different kinds of lettuce and flavors, and cacao powder in perfect harmony with sweet dates—how the addition of bitter makes the dish even more flavorful than without it. So what have we learned? Bitter is good when mixed with other basic tastes.

These raw ingredients are naturally very bitter: leafy greens like arugula, frisée, and endives, kale, Tuscan cabbage, parsley, cacao, and coffee.

UMAMI

Umami is also called the fifth basic taste. It is perhaps the most difficult culinary friend to define. It is sometimes described as being "deep" or "meaty." The same way that bitter signaled to our ancestors a possible poison, sweetness necessary calories, and saltiness needed minerals, umami tells the body that the product contains vital proteins. Animal protein contains lots of umami; it is often this sensation people miss when choosing not to eat animal-based foods entirely or in specific dishes. Umami needs to be there to make up a dish's full taste spectrum. Luckily, there are ingredients in the plant world that contain umami! Onions, a staple in many different dishes worldwide, is a perfect example. Is this a coincidence? I don't believe it is. Algae and soy sauce are other ingredients with plenty of umami. Both have a specifically "deep" taste, one that you perhaps had difficulty to identify before. Now you can—it is umami!

These ingredients are naturally rich in umami: mushrooms, onions, fermented black garlic, tomatoes, miso, celery, algae, tamari, and soy sauce.

10 SUCCESSFUL TASTE COMBINATIONS

- Sweet apricots in a tart tomato soup
- Sweet date, bitter cacao, and salt
- Sour lime and sweet strawberries
- Plain chocolate and salted peanut butter
- Roasted cabbage with nut crumbs and sweet dressing
- Full fat nut dressing seasoned with salt tamari
- Baked sweet potato with tart yogurt sauce and full fat tahini
- Lettuce with roasted sweet root vegetables, arugula, and roasted salted nuts
- Pie with tart apples and a salty caramel sauce
- Noodle soup with miso bouillon and sweet n' spicy tempeh

TEXTURALLY COMPLETE

A creamy soup acquires a more pleasing mouthfeel when topped with a simple quinoa salad bursting with crunch and crispness. For a winter salad of baked soft root vegetables, mix in massaged raw kale or thinly sliced beets.

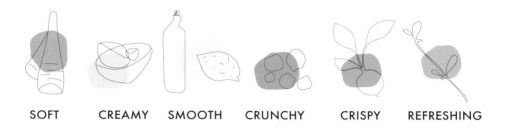

SOFT   CREAMY   SMOOTH   CRUNCHY   CRISPY   REFRESHING

Your meals will go from good to magical; brown bagging goes from a boring necessity to the highlight of the day . . . well, you see where this is heading!

Imagine a plate of creamy carrot purée, topped by a nice soft baked whole sweet carrot, thin strips of orange juice-pickled raw carrot, and a crunchy granola with grated carrot on top. Even if your future dishes aren't going to all look like this, it still gives a clear idea of what texture is all about and how it can be presented on the plate. Finally, yet importantly, it presents a good picture of how one ingredient can, depending on how we prepare and serve it, impart several different textures to a dish. While the five basic flavor sensations are basically set in stone when we mention taste, there is no equivalence for textures. However, I usually use all, or as many as possible, of these six when I cook.

SOFT

Here, "soft" means cooked. All vegetables soften with cooking. How soft they will be depends on the cooking time. Try to add the other textures too, because a plate of all soft foods quickly turns boring and one-dimensional.

Whole oven-baked root vegetables will get a truly delicious soft interior and a slightly crisp exterior if you leave the peel on. Scrub it clean and brush it with oil before baking.

These methods add soft texture to cooked vegetables: oven baked, steamed, fried, or grilled.

CREAMY

Dips are the simplest way to add creaminess to everything, from the breakfast sandwich to the Sunday dinner. Plenty of protein is here if we make the dips using legumes (which are eminently suitable for this purpose). Creamy dips aren't exclusively made from legumes. Baked root vegetables are excellent, too. We usually refer to these as "mash." For a change of pace, add herbs, citrus, flavored cold-pressed oils, and dried mushrooms to your mash.

These ingredients add creamy texture: dips, mash, and smooth soups

SILKY

Sometimes the border between creamy and silky is blurred and all of these textures are usually good on their own. However, it doesn't hurt adding plenty of what's good. I equate silky with dressings and different kinds of marinades. These are generally subtler than creamy dips, staying in the background rather than becoming a more prominent dish component.

These ingredients add silky texture: dressings and marinades

CRUNCH

Crunch is a must-have topping for most dishes. Very little planning is needed here. Just make sure that you always have some toasted seeds or nuts in the pantry, and success is yours, from the breakfast porridge to holiday dessert. There is a huge difference in taste between raw and toasted seeds and nuts. I suggest using toasted; the taste is more pronounced and the texture much more interesting. Even seed crackers add good crunch to a dish.

These ingredients add crunchy texture: toasted seeds, nuts, and whole buckwheat; plain, or mixed into a granola (both sweet and savory kind); mixed nuts, or rye crackers to go with the soup or salad.

CRISP

A handful of thinly shaved raw vegetables is a perfect way to add crispness to your dish. Mix them with some good-quality olive oil and salt to make them milder and softer.

To get an extra crispy edge, leave shaved or cut up beets, other root vegetables, fennel, and radishes (even lettuce leaves) in ice-cold water for about 10 minutes before serving. This is a super trick to wake up most tired-looking vegetables!

These ingredients will add crispness to your raw vegetables: shaved or thinly sliced fennel, carrot, beets, cabbage, or radishes.

FRESHNESS

If you've prepared your dish in advance, add this component at the last moment before serving. Also add it last if you serve from a big batch in the refrigerator over several meals. Mixing in a handful of herbs, tender leafy greens, sprouts, or shoots is often a great way to transform yesterday's leftover gratin or stew into something more exciting.

These ingredients will add freshness: leafy greens like spinach, arugula, or mâche, as well as fresh herbs, sprouts, shoots, and garden cress.

10 SUCCESSFUL TEXTURE COMBINATIONS

- Crisp seed cracker with creamy hummus topped by sprouts
- Raw shaved vegetables mixed into a salad with cooked ingredients
- A crunchy falafel topped with a dollop of silky mayonnaise
- Toasted nuts on silky porridge
- Whole baked, soft celeriac topped with silky nut dressing and crisp root vegetable chips
- Creamy carrot soup topped with quinoa salad with finely chopped vegetables
- Warmed lentil stew topped with cool mint yogurt
- Chewy sourdough bread with silky bean custard and fried mushrooms
- Cooked, chewy spelt with silky carrot custard and crumbled almond feta
- Creamy bean dip topped by chopped herbs in a tomato salsa

See recipe on page 49.

COMPLETE NUTRITION

We need to eat food in order to get all the vital nutrients our bodies require to function: a mixture of carbohydrates, healthy fats, protein, vitamins, and minerals.

CARBOHYDRATES   HEALTHY (GOOD) FATS   PLANT PROTEIN   VITAMINS & MINERALS

Many people wonder if a plant-based or vegan cuisine really can be nutritious enough. The most pressing concern relates to the amount of available protein. So we can continue on our way without worrying needlessly, here is a short summary to answer the more frequent questions. Our food is composed of energy-giving macronutritious proteins, carbohydrates, and fats that all have their own specific characteristics and functions in the body. Different food ingredients contain varying quantities of these macronutrients, but all of them are more or less present in nearly everything we eat. Without giving it a second thought, you're actually getting some protein in each bite you take—even while eating a plant-based diet. Vitamins and minerals are vital for our well-being, and the plant world has an abundance of those!

As long as we know where to look for the plant-based nutrients, know what sources have the highest nutritional value, and eat enough of a varied diet, we are sure to get everything that we need. Not every meal needs to comprise four identifiable sources, but it is a good goal to strive for!

CARBOHYDRATES

"Carbohydrate" is the collective name for starch, dietary fibers, and sugars in the food we eat. We need carbohydrates because they are the body's preferred go-to source for energy. We usually speak about slow and fast acting carbohydrates. This simply means that the slower-acting carbohydrates raise the blood glucose slower. This provides a more even blood glucose curve than quicker-acting carbohydrates, which raise the blood glucose quickly. A slower curve is beneficial for good health. Dietary fibers are carbohydrates that provide an even blood glucose curve, and also have the characteristic of acting as food for the intestinal bacteria. Dietary fibers cannot be digested and are passed down into the colon. This function is extra important because healthy gastrointestinal bacteria and gut flora is vital for both our physical and mental well-being.

These ingredients contain slow-acting carbohydrates and natural dietary fibers: whole grain products, vegetables, root vegetables, fruits, berries, nuts, seeds, and legumes.

HEALTHY (GOOD) FATS

Perhaps you've heard all these different names for fats: polyunsaturated, monounsaturated, saturated, and trans-fats. Fat is a collection of different fatty acids that exist in a combination in the food we eat. Our body needs the right kind of fat to be able to produce hormones, repair cells, and absorb fat-soluble vitamins. In other words, it insures we feel well. The chemical makeup differs between different fats. Fats influence our bodies depending on their makeup; some are better for us (mono and polyunsaturated fats), and others less so. Some fats are even bad for us (saturated and trans-fats). Our goal is to get more of the good healthy fats; reduce the consumption of the bad and unhealthy fats; and altogether stop the consumption of trans-fats. We also need a good balance between the beneficial fats omega-3 and omega-6.

These ingredients contain healthy, good fats: cold-pressed oils, seeds, nuts, and avocados.

PLANT PROTEIN

Protein is the body's building blocks and is needed for, among other things, repairing and building up cells, and creating enzymes and hormones. For protein to do its work, you need to get enough energy (i.e. eat enough calories) depending on your age, gender, and activity level. If there is a calorie deficit, protein will be used to fuel energy instead of being used as a builder. Getting enough protein is really much easier than commonly believed, as nearly everything you eat contains varying amounts of protein.

So what is the difference between plant and animal protein? To understand the difference, we need to start here: A protein molecule is made up of 20 different amino acids. Nine of these are called essential amino acids, because the body cannot produce them and we need to get them from the food we eat. A "complete" protein is called that because it contains a sufficient amount of all nine amino acids that our body needs. Animal proteins are complete proteins, i.e. they contain all nine amino acids. As for vegetable proteins, individual plants don't contain enough of the nine amino acids to make them complete proteins (a few exceptions are soy, buckwheat, and hemp hearts). However, by being savvy and eating a varied diet of plant produce, we can ingest all the amino acids we need in the amounts needed. Different kinds of plant produce contain different kinds of proteins, and therefore different kinds of amino acids. In other words, even plant-based proteins can, without any problem, become complete.

Perhaps you're wondering if those who exercise frequently can satisfy their protein requirement? Of course they can! Just eat more to fill all your (not only protein) nutritional needs. You're probably eating more automatically anyway, if you're very active or training hard, because you are hungrier; by that you're taking in more protein.

These ingredients contain plenty of plant protein: grains/cereals and pseudo grains like buckwheat and quinoa, legumes (even processed products like tofu and tempeh), seeds, and nuts.

VITAMINS AND MINERALS

Our bodies need vitamins and minerals for proper functioning. Vitamins have many important functions, for example to help enzymes (i.e. the substances that start reactions for different activities constantly occurring in the body). Some vitamins have hormone-like characteristics and function like catalysts between different cells. Others help defend the body against free radicals; we call these antioxidants.

Plant-based produce is loaded with vitamins. Those of us who eat a wide variety of plant produce can get, without problems, most of the vital vitamins. The exception is vitamin B12, which needs to be supplemented. Many plant-based products are fortified with vitamin B12. However, depending on how many such products you eat, you may need to add nutritional supplements. If you live in a Nordic country, it may also be a good idea to supplement with vitamin D through the winter months. We don't receive adequate sunlight to supply enough vitamin D during the colder season of the year. Because of this, supplementation is recommended regardless if your diet is wholly plant-based or not.

Minerals exist in varied quantities in all foods. Iodine, iron, and calcium levels are what we usually need to keep an eye on when following a plant-based diet.

Iodine is commonly found not only in seafood, like fish and shellfish, but also in algae. The amount of iodine in algae varies, so it is not a very reliable source. Instead, use natural sea salt, or one with added iodine, to get your iodine need filled. Your plant source for iron is found in foods like whole grains, legumes, seeds, and nuts. Eat a vitamin C-rich plant produce (like white cabbage, citrus, or bell pepper) together with iron-rich plants (like spinach, strawberries, parsley, kale, broccoli, and sesame seeds) to help the body absorb the iron better; and use cast-iron pots when you cook acid-rich foods like tomatoes. You'll find calcium in whole grains, legumes, some nuts and seeds, and also in green leafy vegetables. It's a good idea to add calcium-enriched foods like plant-based beverages and yogurt when you eat those.

Edible plants contain vitamins and minerals. They occur naturally in all plant-based produce.
                        Källa: Johansson, Ulla. Näring och hälsa. 3. Studentlitteratur. Lund 2015.

OVEN-BAKED CELERIAC WITH SMOKED TOFU, SPINACH PESTO, AND PICKLED ONION (recipe accompanies picture on page 45)

Ingredients
1 celeriac root—approx. 2¼ lbs
7 oz smoked tofu
1 tsp olive oil
quick-pickled red onion (see page 108)
watercress

SPINACH PESTO
5 oz fresh spinach
¾ cup pumpkin seeds + ¼ cup for garnish
½ cup cold-pressed olive oil for garnish
1 tbsp fresh organic lemon juice (use zest for garnish)
1 small garlic clove
salt flakes and freshly ground black pepper

How to: Preheat the oven to 395°F (200°C). Clean and scrub the celeriac root thoroughly. Halve the celeriac across and brush it with oil. Bake the root in the oven about 45 to 60 minutes until it is soft straight through. Let it cool and then slice it.

Slice the tofu. Toast the cup of pumpkin seeds in a dry, medium-hot frying pan. Mix the ingredients for the pesto, saving ¼ cup pumpkin seeds for garnish. Season with salt and freshly ground black pepper.

Layer celeriac slices and tofu on a platter. Dot with pesto, and scatter the red onion, pumpkin seeds, and watercress. Drizzle olive oil over. Sprinkle the lot with lemon zest and salt flakes.

A GUIDE: HOW TO PREPARE VEGETABLES

One vegetable has immense possibilities. Vary the meals by preparing the raw ingredients in different ways. You've read this so many times by now it has nearly become a mantra.

The following guide shows several of my favorite ways to prepare some 30 different vegetables. There are also tips on how to serve and vary the vegetables with the help of different dressings, sauces, and other seasonings. These aren't intended to be tips on preparing full-fledged dishes, but instead, as tips on preparing vegetables as part of another dish, a side dish, or as a snack. Many times I don't use exact measurements for ingredients like oil, seasonings, salt, dressings, and other scrumptious things to sprinkle over or use with your vegetables. Follow your taste preferences and let the quantity of vegetables you are preparing guide you. There is no right or wrong here. Let your taste buds show you the way!

The amount you're making, your individual oven, and also your "doneness" preference are all factors that will decide cooking times; nothing is set in stone. Keep an eye on the cooking, and taste test when possible (or check with a toothpick). Let the vegetables soften, but still retain some "chew" to them.

Make it a habit to rinse, brush, and thoroughly clean every ingredient going into a sauce or frying pan, Dutch oven, onto a grill, or into the oven. Unless extremely thick and tough, or you're dealing with a many-layered onion, it's always preferable to leave the peel on. It adds to both the taste and texture.

Different methods

Oven roasting is a very handy way to let the cooking nearly look after itself. It's also very practical for preparing big quantities in one go. Roasting the ingredients will develop deeper flavor, whether you're going to use the vegetables plain or blend them into a soup or dip. When you're roasting vegetables, brush or drizzle them first with some oil, and then sprinkle them with a pinch of salt just before roasting. A conventional oven set at 395°F (200°C) is used for all preparations in this guide unless otherwise suggested. For a convection oven, reduce the temperature 25°F below the suggested conventional oven temperature.

A good way to quickly cook thinly sliced vegetables is to wok or pan-fry them. These methods develop an appetizing exterior. Many kinds of onions and mushrooms come into their own when fried. The same goes for the classic potato pancake [latke], a dish that can easily be made from other vegetables, too. Grilling vegetables, either on skewers or in a grill wok, will give nearly the same result as frying.

Steaming is another favorite method. Steam the vegetables only until they are softened but still have some bite left. I like this method because it is extremely quick and a great way to cook while retaining a maximum of nutrition. Steaming suits most vegetables (with the exception of mushrooms, onions, and zucchini, which get water-logged and mushy), and they are best served mixed with a good dressing (for recipes, see page 99). Another way to serve steamed vegetables is by mashing with some salt, herbs, and perhaps some lemon juice and zest. Go ahead and season mashed oven-roasted or steamed vegetables with salt and perhaps herbs, some miso, a spice mix, or pesto rosso as an alternative.

Remember, these are just some suggestions. Start with these and then add your own preparations as you go along.

Uniformity

For oven roasting, to make sure that everything is done at the same time, it's a good idea to cut vegetables into evenly sized pieces or add certain vegetables toward the end of the cooking time. Whole vegetables need longer than cut-up pieces. Root vegetables usually need longer cooking time than other vegetables such as cabbage, green beans, and zucchini.

Warm or cold-pressed oil

If something needs to be brushed or tossed with oil before cooking, we recommend a neutral tasting, warm-pressed oil (for example canola). These oils have a higher smoking point. Cold-pressed canola or olive oil is used in dressings and sauces, or to drizzle over dishes, both for flavor and nutritional value.

TIP

Sprinkle nutritional yeast [not brewer's yeast] over roasting vegetables, or massage cabbage leaves with the yeast when making chips. It'll give them a great cheese flavor!

All cabbage leaves are suitable for chip-making. Try out Brussels sprouts, thinly shredded Savoy cabbage, and cauliflower greens.

KALE—BLACK/ TUSCAN CABBAGE

Oven bake

Preheat the oven to 305°F (150°C). Tear the leaves into smaller pieces, massage them with some oil, and salt until all are covered. Without them touching, place the pieces on a baking sheet and roast until the pieces are dry and crisp. This will take approximately 7 to 10 minutes.

Steam

Tear the leaves into smaller pieces and then steam them for 1 minute. Remove the leaves from the heat and massage them with a good-quality cold-pressed oil or a dressing.

Massage

Shred the leaves finely. Massage the shreds thoroughly with some oil and salt, or a dressing, until they are softened. It is also nice to add finely shredded kale and Tuscan cabbage to lentil or hearty root vegetable stews. Add the shreds as you remove the stew from the heat.

WHITE CABBAGE— BULL-HEART (POINTY/ SWEETHEART) CABBAGE

Oven bake

Cut the cabbage into wedges and brush them with oil. Bake the wedges for about 20 to 30 minutes until edges are softened, golden, and slightly crispy. Serve them drizzled with dressing (choose from page 99) and some toasted nuts or seeds.

Fry

Finely shred the cabbage. Fry in oil together with freshly grated ginger and finely grated garlic until the cabbage is soft and slightly golden in color. Season with salt and freshly ground pepper.

Massage

Shred the raw cabbage very fine and massage it with a good-quality oil and some salt, or with dressing, until the cabbage is soft. Serve the cabbage in a salad, in a wrap, on a sandwich, or in a soup for a nice crispy texture.

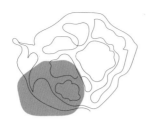

CAULIFLOWER

Oven-bake

Whole: Place the cauliflower in an ovenproof dish. Bake the cauliflower for 45 to 60 minutes until it is golden and crisp on the exterior, but soft straight through the interior. Serve it plain or grate it into cauliflower rice. The shorter baking time is fine if you are planning on ricing the cauliflower.

Florets: Break the cauliflower into florets. Place them on a baking sheet and sprinkle with garlic powder. Bake for about 20 to 25 minutes until they are crispy around the edges.

Pizza crust

Finely grate a large head of cauliflower. Pour the shreds into a saucepan filled with boiling water and then immediately drain. Let cool and then thoroughly press out the water. Mix 2 tablespoons of chia seeds in ½ cup boiling water and let it stand for 5 minutes. This will make two chia "eggs." Make the dough out of the grated cauliflower, chia "eggs," 1 tablespoon of psyllium husk, ½ cup almond flour, and ½ teaspoon salt. On a baking sheet, press the dough into a flat round. Bake for about 20 minutes. Remove the crust from the oven and top the crust with your choice of topping (try one of the nut cheeses on page 109) and bake for another few minutes until the topping has softened and colored nicely. *Tip!* Double the recipe for four servings.

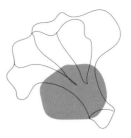

BROCCOLI

BROCCOLI

Cut the broccoli, separate into florets, and slice the stem into coins. Toss the broccoli in some oil and garlic powder, and then place the pieces on a baking sheet. Bake for about 7 minutes until the broccoli is crisp around the edges.

Steam

Cut the broccoli, separate it into florets, and slice the stem into coins. Steam the pieces for 2 to 3 minutes and then rinse under running cold water. Drizzle the broccoli with a tasty dressing and sprinkle over a good pinch of salt flakes. This is a great side dish that goes with everything!

Some more options

Quick fry or grill: Cut the broccoli, separate it into florets, and slice the stem into coins. Fry the pieces in some oil (or brush with oil and grill) until the florets get an appetizing look. Serve them together with a miso or tamari-flavored mayonnaise (see recipe on page 99). Broccolini is superb prepared this way.

BRUSSELS SPROUTS

Oven-bake

Trim off the base of the stalk and cut the cabbage heads in half. Brush them with oil and a pinch of salt. Bake them about 7 to 10 minutes, until the cabbages are slightly crispy around the edges but the center is still chewy. Drizzle a tart dressing and fresh herbs over and add finely chopped apple.

Steam

Trim off the base and cut the cabbage heads in half. Steam the heads for 5 to 7 minutes, until they have softened but the center is still chewy. Rinse the heads with cold water to stop the cooking. Mix the cabbages with a dressing of your choice.

Massage

Slice the cabbage head finely with a mandoline. Massage thoroughly with some oil and salt (or use a dressing) until the cabbage slices are softened; do this preferably together with other kinds of cabbage. The cabbage will work as a tasty base for salads, to add a crisp texture in a wrap, as a simple green cabbage salad, or a green side dish.

PUMPKIN/SQUASH

Oven-bake

Halve the squash and brush the cut surface with oil. Bake the halves for 45 minutes. You can also cut the squash into wedges or small cubes and bake them for 15 to 25 minutes. Drizzle the squash with dressing or toss with a spice mix. Serve as a complement or in a salad or wrap.

Steam

Cut the squash in small cubes. Steam the cubes for 10 minutes. Rinse the cubes under cold water. Together with herbs, some cold-pressed canola oil, and lemon, purée the squash into a mash.

Some more options

Pickling: Grate coarsely and mix with the pickling liquid on page 108.
Crudité: Spiralized or julienned (read more about this utensil on page 31), squash provides flavorful crunch in salads.
Stews: Cube the squash and add the cubes to lentil or other kinds of stews.

ZUCCHINI

Oven-bake

Slice the zucchini in half lengthwise. Scoop the flesh from both halves and chop it coarsely. Mix in chopped walnuts, minced garlic, cooked chickpeas or lentils, two handfuls of fresh herbs, salt and pepper—or use leftover salad fixings. Top the whole with almond feta (see recipe on page 109). Bake in the oven for 20 minutes.

Fry

Slice the zucchini thinly and sauté in a frying pan with some oil and chopped garlic until the zucchini is golden brown and soft. Season with salt and freshly ground pepper. Mix in chopped herbs and remove from the heat.

Spiralize

Raw: Spiralize the zucchini and serve it in place of noodles, or together with noodles in a soup or salad. Slice thinly and use as a refreshing base for a summer salad. Roulades: Plane the zucchini thinly lengthwise. Fill the slices with a mixture of chopped mushrooms, walnuts, and cooked lentils and then roll up. Place the roulades in an ovenproof dish, cover with tomato sauce, and bake until the roulades are soft. Try layering with eggplant slices!

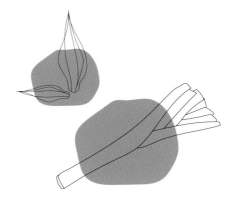

ONIONS

Oven-bake

Peel and cut the onion into wedges (or julienne thinly if you use leeks). Place the onion in an oven-proof dish and bake about 20 minutes until soft. Onions are great as part of a baking sheet full of roasted root vegetables.

Fry

Peel the onion and cut into small wedges. Heat a frying pan, cover the bottom with water, and let the onion blanch until soft. Drizzle over some oil and continue to sauté over low heat until the onion is caramelized. Caramelized onions are great together with rustic meals or as a base for stew or soup. Try letting a splash of balsamic vinegar cook with the caramelized onion.

Some more options

Pickling: you'll find how to do this on page 108.
Umami-bomb: It is not by chance that onions (and often garlic) are the base for myriads of dishes the world over. How come? They provide the dish with a certain delicious flavor "depth." Finely chopped onion fried in some oil until soft is a good starting block for just about any dish: stews, soups, vegetable burgers, gratins, risotto—the list goes on!

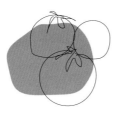

TOMATO

Oven-bake

Preheat the oven to 305°F (150°C). Place wedges from large tomatoes or whole branches of cherry tomatoes in an ovenproof dish. Drizzle with some cold-pressed oil, add a splash of red wine or apple cider vinegar, a pinch of salt, and some fresh thyme. Bake for about 45 minutes until the tomatoes have shrunk. Bake a few unpeeled cloves of garlic with the tomatoes for interest. Press out the soft-baked garlic cloves and mix with the tomato juice. Drizzle the juice over the dish at serving time.

Semi-dried

Preheat the oven to 260°F (125°C). Halve the tomatoes and brush on some oil. Place the halves on a rimmed baking sheet and slow roast them for about 75 to 90 minutes, until the edges are crisp and the tomatoes semi-dry.

Tomato salad

Thinly slice different shaped and sized vine-ripened tomatoes and arrange them on a platter. Top the slices with dollops of cashew ricotta (see the recipe on page 109), sourdough croutons, and drizzles of olive oil—preferably flavored (lemon or garlic for example)—and freshly chopped basil.

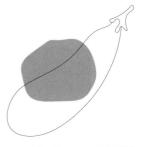

EGGPLANT

Oven-bake

Slice or halve the eggplant and brush the cut surfaces with olive oil. Bake the slices approximately 25 to 30 minutes. Alternatively, cube the eggplant and drizzle with finely chopped garlic, some oil, and a pinch of salt before baking them for about 20 minutes.

Steam

This is a quick version of the baba ghanoush dip: Cut the eggplant in half and steam the pieces for 10 minutes. Spoon out the inside, purée it with lemon, tahini, garlic, and mint into a creamy dip (you'll see the full recipe on page 103).

Some more options

Roulades: Check out the recipe under "Zucchini." **Holiday dips:** Fried eggplant gets a texture that is creamy, but with a slight bite to it. This makes it very handy and good to add to other kinds of dips that are served traditionally at Midsummer and Christmas holidays. Think of mustardy eggplant, basil eggplant—I'm sure you can name your own favorite! Cut the eggplant into smaller pieces, sprinkle over some salt, and let it sit for 10 minutes to draw out some water. Fry the eggplant pieces in some oil until they are soft inside but crisp on the outside. Cover them with your favorite sauce!

PEAS—GREEN BEANS

Sautéing

Fry finely chopped garlic in some oil until the garlic is aromatic. Fold in the beans and/or peas and fry until they soften some, but still retain some bite. Sprinkle with chili flakes, fresh herbs, and salt flakes.

Steam

Steam peas/beans for 5 to 7 minutes. Rinse under cold water to stop the cooking.

Crudité

Julienne thinly lengthwise and serve them raw in a salad or wrap. Add some lemon juice and salt as a flavor enhancer, or add to a hummus bowl for a delicious and crispy topping.

In a stew: It is better to buy frozen peas and beans during the part of the year when you can't find fresh produce. The frozen ingredients are mostly suited for chopping up and adding to stews and wok dishes. *Tip!* Examples of garden beans and peas are: snap beans, haricots verts, yellow wax beans, string beans, sugar peas, and sugar snap peas.

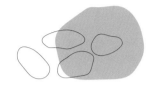

POTATOES

Oven-bake

Bake them whole (about 35 to 45 minutes), in wedges (25 to 30 minutes), or in thin slices (15 to 20 minutes) until the peel is golden and slightly crisp.

Boil

Rinse and scrub them thoroughly. If necessary, cut larger potatoes down to get more uniform pieces. Barely cover the potatoes with lightly salted water and boil them, with a lid on the pan, for about 20 minutes. A good way to prepare potatoes is by adding mustard to make a spicy mash or coarsely riced potatoes.

Some more options

Potato chips: Preheat the oven to 305°F (150°C). Slice potatoes very thinly with a mandoline. Cover the slices with some oil and a pinch of salt. Let them rest for about 15 minutes. Drain off any liquid that has collected. Place the slices in a single layer, without touching, on a baking sheet and bake for about 45 to 60 minutes. Open the oven door a few times to release the steam. Let cool.

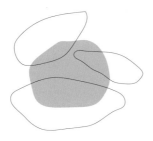

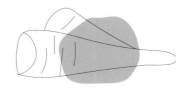

SWEET POTATOES

Oven-bake

With a knife, cut an X on the upper side of a whole potato and bake it around 45 to 60 minutes. Alternately, cut it into large wedges and bake for about 25 to 30 minutes, or cut into small cubes and bake for about 15 to 20 minutes. To get crispy "french fries," cut strips, rinse with water, and dry the strips with a kitchen towel. Brush the strips with oil, place them in a single layer on a baking sheet, and bake them for about 30 minutes.

Steam

Cut the sweet potato into small cubes. Steam them for 10 minutes. Mix them with your choice of dressing or sauce. You can also mash the cubes.

Speed toasting

Slice the sweet potato thinly and toast the slices in the toaster—the world's quickest way to prepare sweet potato slices. Top them with a simple salad and drizzle a tasty dressing over it all.

PARSNIP

Oven

Bake them whole (about 30 to 40 minutes) until they have softened and the surface is golden and slightly crisp. Try also to bake large parsnip pieces (about 25 minutes) or thin slices (about 15 minutes).

Steam

Cut the parsnip into small cubes. Steam them for about 10 minutes. Mix the steamed parsnip cubes with your choice of dressing or sauce, or just mash them.

Some more options

Chips: see instructions above for how to make potato chips.
Bread: Mix grated parsnip into the scone dough (see recipe on page 104), the muffin or cake batter (think carrot cake but replace it with parsnip). Finely grated parsnip is also nice in home-made granola, as it imparts a touch of natural sweetness.
Lentil stew: Parsnip adds a nice flavor, some sweetness, and soft consistency to the stew. Cut parsnip into smaller pieces and let them cook with the stew.

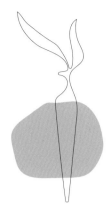

CARROT

Oven

Bake carrots whole in the oven for 35 to 45 minutes until softened and the outside is golden and slightly crisp. If the carrots are cut into large chunks, 25 to 30 minutes will suffice. Try them also thinly sliced and bake for about 15 minutes.

Steam

Cut the carrots into small dice. Steam them for about 10 minutes. Rinse with cold water and then add them to a sauce or dressing of your choice. Or why not just mash them?

Julienne or spiralize

Pickle: Grate coarsely and mix with the pickling liquid on page 108.
Crudité: Spiralize or use a julienne peeler to make thin strips (see more on page 31), which give a nice crunch to salads.

BEETS

Oven

Bake the beets whole for about 45 minutes, in wedges for about 30 to 35 minutes, or diced for about 20 to 25 minutes. Preferably separate the beets if you do red, yellow, and Chioggia beets together, as the beets will stain otherwise.

Steam

Cut the beets into wedges. Steam them for 15 minutes. Mix the beets with a nice dressing, some crunchy nuts, and fresh herbs.

More options

Beet chips: Prepare as for potato chips. Cut off the beet tops and hold the beets by the bottom when you slice them.
Raw slice: Thin slices add appetizing crunch to salads.

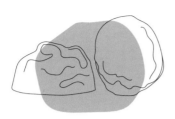

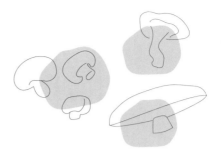

CELERIAC

Oven

Scrub the celeriac thoroughly and cut off any dirty sections. Brush the celeriac with oil. Bake it on a rack positioned in the middle of the oven for about 60 to 70 minutes, until the root is soft straight through. Serve the root sliced, grated into smaller pieces, or slice thinly to use on a sandwich.

You can also dice the celeriac and mix the dice with oil and a pinch of salt. Bake for 25 to 35 minutes.

Steam

Dice the celeriac finely and steam for about 10 minutes. Mix the dice with a sauce or dressing of your choice; or just mash them.

More options

Celeriac pancake: Mix 3½ cups of coarsely grated celeriac, ¾ cup chickpea flour, 2½ fl oz water, a pinch of salt, and a handful of chopped parsley. Let the mixture rest 10 minutes. Dot out small pancakes in an oiled frying pan and fry until the pancake is crisp and golden on both sides. Serve with a dip from page 103.

MUSHROOMS

Oven

Most mushrooms taste best if they are slightly crisp. Therefore, if you have baked them in the oven, give them a quick crisping-up in an oiled, hot frying pan before serving. Portabella mushrooms are excellent when baked whole, brushed with tamari or soy sauce. To serve, slice or use them as "burgers."

Fry

All kinds of mushrooms are good fried to a light golden color and a slightly crisp surface. Start off without oil until all liquid disappears, and then drizzle over some oil and fry until the mushrooms have some color.

Mushrooms meant for the freezer need to be blanched first. Let their liquid evaporate in the frying pan together with a pinch of salt.

Pickle with spice or dehydrate

Pickle in spice: see recipe on page 108. You can dehydrate mushrooms if you have an abundance of them. Rehydrate the mushrooms in water for about 30 minutes before using.

THE PLANT-BASED FORMULA

BYE, BYE "HEALTHY EATING PLATE"

Plant-based food differs in many ways from other types of cuisine and from many traditional dishes, which are frequently built according to the "healthy eating plate" model. This "healthy eating plate" is divided into a protein source, which is (more often than not) animal-based + a carbohydrate source + a vegetable side. A plant-based meal isn't necessarily divided into three disconnected parts because it is composed as a whole, regardless of what kind of dishes we talk about.
In these recipes, several, or perhaps all ingredients may add protein, fat, and carbohydrates. Instead of having to follow three main nutritional components, a plant-based dish can easily be built around one or two specific ingredients. In order to create that whole, we also make sure to include flavors, colors, textures, and nutrition, which are needed to get a really delectable and perfectly satisfying dish. Sounds a bit unfamiliar? Possibly. Simple as can be? Absolutely!

HELLO PLANT-BASED PLATE

Within a few pages you'll find a collection of formulas that simplify your work putting together different kinds of plant-based dishes. Hopefully the formulas will help you from day one. I think we can call the formulas our "trusted kitchen companions." What is so extraordinary is, with the help of these companions, a whole new world will open up to you—just wait and see!

Plant-based cooking is a new, contemporary way to approach food preparation for anyone who loves food. Our intention is to give you a solid foundation, helping you to transform into a dynamic cook willing and able to experiment in the kitchen. Instead of spelling out exact ingredient lists meant to be followed to a T, we break down a dish into its components, clarifying what makes the dish so good and satisfying. Because ingredients are going to vary according to seasonal availability, your refrigerator might have a different look from week to week. Sometimes, you may face the dilemma of making do with very few ingredients, so isn't it smarter to learn how we *build a dish* before we look at detailed recipes? It's a bit like building a sturdy house before we pick out the wallpaper.

Plants are more than vegetables

Eating a plant-based diet mustn't confine us to consuming exclusively vegetables. The plant kingdom is brimming with ingredients like nuts, seeds, and many kinds of legumes and grains. Let's not forget spices, herbs, and other flavorings as well. Plant-based dishes aren't just the vegetables we see above ground, the roots, and leafy greens. In fact, this cuisine has everything you need to create delicious and hearty dishes for all meals. Sometimes I hear people say, "I don't feel satiated when I only eat vegetables." There is a universal solution for this: Just eat more.

Plant tapas

A fun way to serve vegetables, apart from in main course meals, is to prepare one or a pair separately, letting them come into their own and shine. Let's call them plant tapas. Serve them simply with a nice dressing or sauce and a crunchy topping. Add some lentils or other legumes to make a more filling version. Pair a couple of sliced oven-baked beets with a yogurt dressing and a sprinkle of toasted seeds. Take hummus flavored with roasted carrot and drizzle it with a good-quality olive oil. Oven-baked cauliflower florets can be turned into a tart gremolata. Toss together thinly sliced fennel with apple. You'll have a luxurious dinner in no time at all. All this made from vegetables that, at first glance, looked rather uninspiring!

Below are a few samples of how quickly combined plant tapas might look:

5 VEGETABLE TAPAS

- Baked beets—yogurt sauce—nut and kale crumbs

- Roasted carrots—carrot top pesto—massaged Brussels sprouts—pistachios

- Beefsteak tomato—herb oil—cabbage and bread crumbs

- Baked eggplant—miso dressing and plant yogurt—dukka

- Steamed young vegetables—gremolata—plant yogurt—chickpea croutons

FROM PLANT MODEL TO PLATE OF PLEASURE

Talking about the plant-based model is all very well, but how do you practice it? Well, look and see how I used the plant model as a foundation ("How to Build a Dish") and developed formulas for four different kinds of dishes. I call these the "ultimate formulas" because they fundamentally assist you in making delicious, complete, and exciting dishes instantly. You will get *ultimate formulas* for:

Salads and bowls
Sandwiches
Hummus bowls
Porridge

Perhaps you wonder why we've chosen these particular dishes. Well, quite simply, they are exceptionally tasty and versatile dishes.

HOW TO READ THE FORMULAS

We'll begin with an introduction to the type of dish we are going to prepare; a presentation of the different categories building this type of dish; and how the categories contribute to just this dish.

Following each formula, I have put together five combinations based on everything you've just learned. I particularly like these matches because they use what I have on hand alongside seasonal products. They can often contain more than one part from each category. There is a picture of the finished dishes at the beginning of each formula. There are no detailed cooking instructions for the different components, as the purpose is to get your creative juices flowing. If you need tips on various ways to prepare the vegetables, check out the guide on pages 50 to 51. You'll find recipes for dips on page 103, toppings on page 109, and dressings on page 99.

SALADS AND BOWLS

Grains/noodles + 2–4 basic vegetables + legume + leafy greens + dip/dressing + 1–2 toppings

It's very simple to throw together both generous and enticing salads and bowls by following the above formula. Go ahead and pick something from each category to make the meals luscious and satisfying.

In addition to being consumed as individual servings, salads are the perfect choice for buffet meals or when you have to feed a larger gathering. Salads can be prepared mostly in advance and they are ideal for serving at room temperature. If you're offering a selection of assorted salads for your buffet or dinner party, individually they won't need to contain ingredients from every category listed below. Preferably, create a mix of salads and tapas, each composed of a few select ingredient categories. So, when added up, you arrive at the overall "whole" you're striving for.

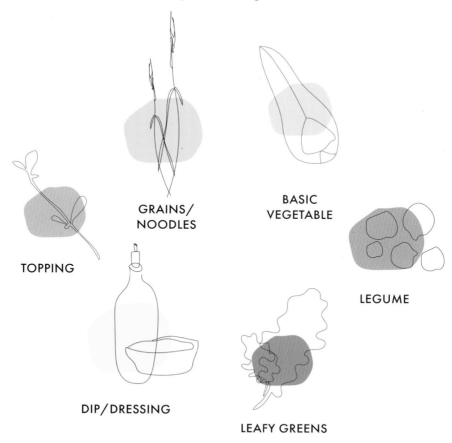

TOPPING

GRAINS/
NOODLES

BASIC
VEGETABLE

LEGUME

DIP/DRESSING

LEAFY GREENS

THE ULTIMATE FORMULA: SALADS AND BOWLS

GRAINS/NOODLES

This is a substantial base. Cook your grains plain or you can add ginger/saffron/turmeric or a splash of coconut milk for variety. You might consider swapping half the grains/noodles for riced vegetables or vegetable noodles, i.e. spiralized or grated raw vegetables.

2–4 BASE VEGETABLES

These are the heart of your salad. Try to choose seasonal produce. Varying the preparation will add more interest to your vegetables; perhaps oven-bake one and grate another. Below are just a few examples, but go to the guide on page 50 for more ways how to cook them.

LEGUMES

Serve them cooked plain, together with a tasty dressing, shaped into falafel or burgers and baked, made into tofu or tempeh (check page 119 for tips on how to prepare), or why not make a creamy dip?

Sorghum/millet

Quinoa: red, white, black

Oat: whole-grain or intact oat kernels, complete with bran

Spelt

Barley

Durra

Wild rice

Rice: brown, red, black

Vegetable noodles or vegetable rice (try roasted cauliflower and mix to rice consistency)

Pumpkin

Carrot

Parsnip

Celeriac

Brussels sprouts

Fennel

Zucchini

Tomato

Mushrooms: oyster, portabella, chanterelles, button mushrooms, shiitake

---

Beans: black, white, fava, kidney, edamame

Peas: chickpeas, yellow, green

Lentils: Beluga, red, green, Gotland, Le Puy

Tofu

Tempeh

Ground soy meat substitute

LEAFY GREENS

When preparing coarse leaves like kale or Tuscan cabbage, massage them with some oil and a pinch of salt to soften them and make their flavor milder. More delicate leaves like spinach, arugula, and mâche can go directly into the salad.

DIP/DRESSING & SAUCES

Sometimes, offering a single dip or dressing is enough, but you can never go wrong having several. Dips make dishes more filling and entertaining. They can be made from legumes, vegetables, or a combination. You'll find all the recipes for the items below on pages 99 to 103.

1–2 TOPPINGS

Toasted nuts or spicy seed mixtures get you that little bit of extra freshness and crunch with an additional flavor punch. You'll find several of the suggestions on page 109.

Leafy Greens	Dip/Dressing & Sauces	1–2 Toppings
Spinach	Baba ghanoush with loads of lemon	Fresh herbs
Mâche	Baked carrot dip with miso and ginger	Seeds or nuts, raw or toasted with a spice mixture
Arugula	White bean dip with roasted garlic and thyme	Nut and kale crumbs
Romaine (Cos) lettuce	Crushed pea and cucumber dip with cumin and plant-based yoghurt	Sauerkraut
Frisé lettuce	Herb hummus	Pickled red onion or cucumber
Chard	Roasted carrot hummus	Salt mixes: dukka, furikake, Nordic winter mix
Cabbage shoots: kale, Tuscan cabbage	Almond sauce	Deep-fried garlic
Massaged cabbage: kale, Tuscan cabbage, Brussels sprouts	Pumpkin seed vinaigrette	Almond feta
Fresh herbs	Libyan Chraime sauce	Pesto rosso
Sprouts and shoots		

THESS SUGGESTS

Salads come in a multitude of costumes; I call all tasty combinations of different vegetables a salad. I often have several different salad fixings ready in my refrigerator and freezer, because once I start preparing I frequently batch cook. It is so simple that way to throw together bowls of goodies at the drop of a hat—both on weekdays and for special occasions. This also makes it easy to serve several persons with different needs and preferences. What ends up in the bowl today depends on the season, what I already have on hand, and what my current craving prods me to make.

	CEREALS/NOODLES		2–4 BASE VEGETABLES		LEGUMES
1.	Quinoa	→	Roasted pumpkin, red onion, Brussels sprouts	→	Almond marinated chickpeas
2.	Spelt	→	Massaged Tuscan cabbage + white cabbage and roasted potatoes with pumpkin seed dressing	→	Green pea hummus
3.	Wild rice	→	Roasted parsnip + portabella	→	Smoked tofu
4.	Durra	→	Semi-dried tomatoes, roasted cauliflower, julienned sugar snap peas	→	Falafel
5.	Soba noodles	→	Julienned carrots + garlic-roasted broccoli	→	Sweet 'n spicy peanut tempeh

1. Quinoa salad with roasted squash, Brussels sprouts, marinated chickpeas, and almond sauce
2. Spelt salad with massaged cabbage salad, roasted potatoes, pumpkin seed vinaigrette, and green pea hummus
3. Wild rice salad with roasted parsnip, portabella, smoked tofu, miso dressing, and almond feta
4. Durra salad with roasted cauliflower, semi-dried tomatoes, carrot falafel, and baked carrot dip
5. Soba noodles with carrot, garlic roasted broccoli, peanut tempeh, turmeric and tahini dressing, and roasted peanuts

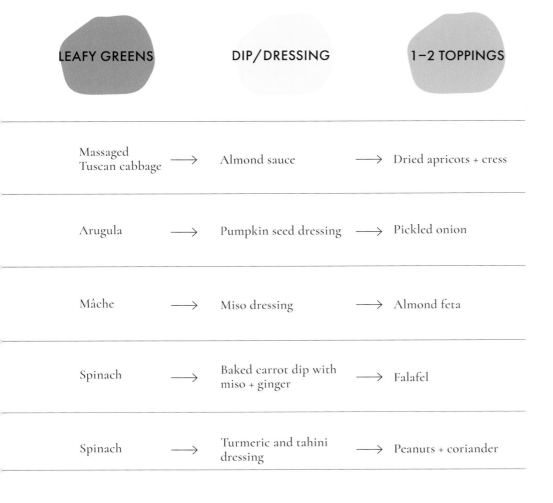

LEAFY GREENS	DIP/DRESSING	1–2 TOPPINGS
Massaged Tuscan cabbage ⟶	Almond sauce ⟶	Dried apricots + cress
Arugula ⟶	Pumpkin seed dressing ⟶	Pickled onion
Mâche ⟶	Miso dressing ⟶	Almond feta
Spinach ⟶	Baked carrot dip with miso + ginger ⟶	Falafel
Spinach ⟶	Turmeric and tahini dressing ⟶	Peanuts + coriander

SANDWICHES

Bread/crackers + leafy greens + dip, custard or nut butter or tofu or chickpea scramble + 1–2 vegetables or salad base + 1–2 toppings

A sandwich or wrap can stand in for any meal during the day. Sandwiches are perfect as part of a buffet at a mingle event, if served in individual forms. If served as a snack or part of a breakfast it's enough to choose from the categories below. However, if it's intended to be a substantial meal, it is good to add an extra topping. I'll give suggestions for both simple and more robust sandwiches on pages 76 to 79. It's very easy to make your own plant-based sandwich fillings by roasting whole root vegetables. Beets, celeriac, and carrots are some of my favorites. They should first be scrubbed thoroughly before roasting. After cleaning, brush them all over with oil and bake them in a 350°F (175°C) oven until soft straight through. Then, just slice them thinly. Even store-bought smoked tofu, when sliced thinly, is a savory filling in either a sandwich or a wrap.

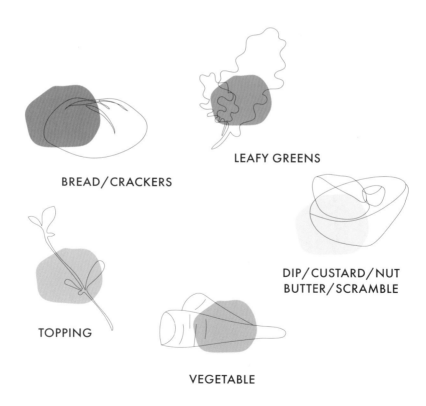

BREAD/CRACKERS

LEAFY GREENS

DIP/CUSTARD/NUT BUTTER/SCRAMBLE

TOPPING

VEGETABLE

THE ULTIMATE FORMULA: SANDWICHES

BREAD

Make a habit of keeping slices of nice sourdough in your freezer. You'll have them on hand for a quick warm-up in the oven resulting in a just-baked taste! Rye crackers are another handy staple; they can be served with nourishing toppings and also as a snack with a tasty dip.

LEAFY GREENS

Creamy textures need a bit of freshness. Leafy greens and raw, massaged cabbage leaves—scrumptious when mixed with a delicious dressing—make good sandwich or wrap fillings because they create interesting and subtle differences in texture.

DIP/CUSTARD/NUT BUTTER/SCRAMBLE

A creamy texture is the objective here. The ingredients can vary, so we give several suggestions below. With a nut or seed butter handy, you're always ready to roll. Dips, custards, and scrambles made from chickpeas, tofu, or tempeh are highly nutritious and pleasing.

Sourdough bread (see recipe on page 106)

Sourdough rolls

Seed bread

Potato flatbread (see recipe on page 104)

Lentil crackers (see recipe on page 104)

Rye bread

Scones (see recipe on page 104)

Spinach

Mâche

Arugula

Romaine lettuce

Frisé lettuce

Chard shoots, cabbage shoots: kale, Tuscan cabbage

Massaged cabbage: kale, Tuscan cabbage, Brussels sprouts

Fresh herbs

Sprouts and shoots

Tofu scramble (see recipe on page 115)

Chickpea scramble (see recipe on page 116)

Baba ghanoush (see recipe on page 103)

Baked carrot custard with miso (see recipe on page 103)

Different flavored hummus

Cashew ricotta

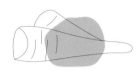

1–2 VEGETABLES

Sometimes just a dip and some leafy greens is enough, especially if it is to go with a tofu scramble. However, if serving sandwiches for lunch, some extra vegetables add a layer of flavor and make your meal more substantial.

Tomato, baked or raw

Baked celeriac or beets, thinly sliced

Salsa—especially tomato and cucumber—suits the warmer months

Spiralized vegetables like carrots, zucchini, and beets

Lettuce

Mushrooms: pickled/fermented, fried, or baked

1–2 TOPPINGS/ FLAVORINGS

If desired, these bring crowning flavor and texture. I don't leave the choices at just herbs or pickled vegetables, but also "plant-based fillings." For example: thinly sliced pieces of smoked tofu or oven-baked root vegetables.

Toasted nuts or seeds

Pickled red onion or cucumber

Sauerkraut

Herbs

Mayonnaise

Plant-based fillings like oven-baked beets, celeriac, or carrot

Deep-fried garlic

Nut cheese

THESS SUGGESTS

I always have a few sliced loaves of good bread stashed away in the freezer, and now and then, even a freshly-baked spelt sourdough loaf on the kitchen counter. This way, I can always retrieve the exact number of slices I need for the moment. Sometimes the bread is a side, other times it's the star of the meal. A hearty, flavorful loaf doesn't really need a lot of gussying up. Sourdough, freshly out of the oven, drizzled with quality cold-pressed olive oil and a pinch of salt flakes, can hold its own. Still, using the formula on the previous page, I layer or fill the sandwich with goodies when I desire more of a meal. This is how it might look:

	BREAD		LEAFY GREENS		DIP/CUSTARD/NUT BUTTER/SCRAMBLE
1.	Sourdough bread	$\longrightarrow$	Mâche lettuce	$\longrightarrow$	Cashew ricotta
2.	Sourdough bread	$\longrightarrow$	Lettuce and pumpkin seed dressing	$\longrightarrow$	Hummus with herbs
3.	Potato flatbread	$\longrightarrow$	Mixed lettuce	$\longrightarrow$	Chickpea scramble
4.	Lentil crackers	$\longrightarrow$		$\longrightarrow$	Vegan seafood
5.	Rye bread	$\longrightarrow$	Spinach	$\longrightarrow$	Pesto rosso

1. Spelt sourdough sandwich with cashew ricotta, pickled mushrooms, and sprouts
2. Spelt sourdough sandwich with herb-flavored hummus, lettuce with pumpkin seed dressing, oven-baked tomatoes, and cress
3. Potato flatbread with chickpea scramble, pickled red onion, and dukkah
4. Lentil crackers with vegan seafood and cress
5. Rye bread with pesto rosso, spinach, and smoked tofu

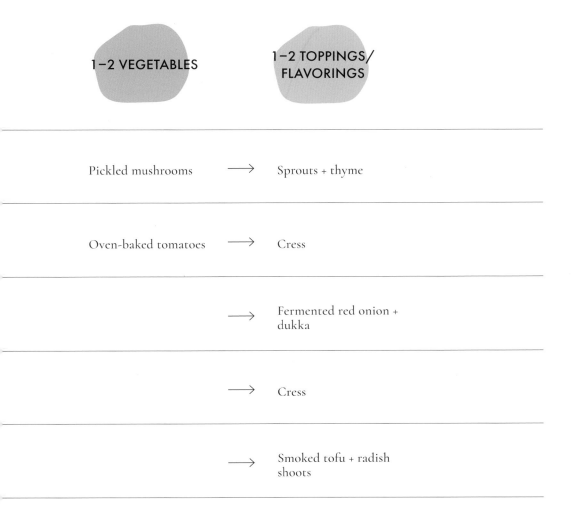

1–2 VEGETABLES   **1–2 TOPPINGS/ FLAVORINGS**

Pickled mushrooms $\longrightarrow$ Sprouts + thyme

Oven-baked tomatoes $\longrightarrow$ Cress

$\longrightarrow$ Fermented red onion + dukka

$\longrightarrow$ Cress

$\longrightarrow$ Smoked tofu + radish shoots

HUMMUS BOWLS

Legume + seed, almond or nut butter + flavoring
1–3 vegetables + leafy greens + (optional) dressing + 1–2 toppings

Hummus is more than just a small side dish; it's also a substantial starter for sharing. Page 87 has a basic recipe for hummus, and you can experiment by replacing the chickpeas with other legumes like yellow or green peas, white beans, or cooked red lentils. You can complete a creamy hummus quickly by combining leftovers from the refrigerator and freezer. Finish it with grilled tomatoes, gremolata, and some toasted seeds served with rustic sourdough bread. During the warmer season, add vine-ripe tomatoes and a handful of leafy greens together with toasted nuts.

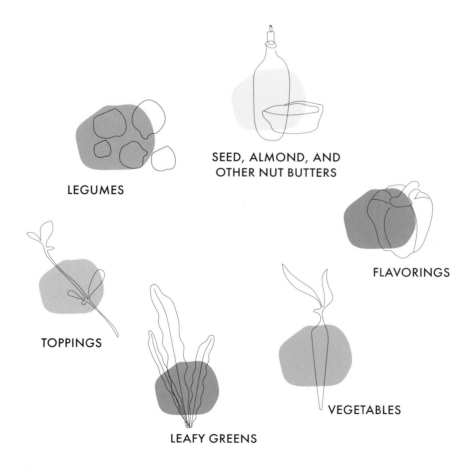

LEGUMES

SEED, ALMOND, AND
OTHER NUT BUTTERS

FLAVORINGS

TOPPINGS

LEAFY GREENS

VEGETABLES

THE ULTIMATE FORMULA: HUMMUS BOWLS

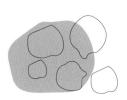 

LEGUMES

Although a classic hummus is made from chickpeas, I use a lot of different plants like cooked lentils, beans, and peas to make creamy dips. I always make sure to whip up an extra large batch because hummus is the perfect side dish.

SEED/NUT BUTTERS

This ingredient is needed to make a dip exceptionally creamy. Tahini made from sesame seeds is the most common plant butter, but it's enjoyable and fun to experiment with other kinds of nut butters. Count on 1 tablespoon of nut or seed butter for each ½ lb. (drained) container of cooked legumes. 1 tablespoon cold-pressed oil works in a pinch, too.

1–2 FLAVORINGS

Flavorings can be a spice or spice mixes, vegetables, or herbs. Do you have leftovers of roasted root vegetables from yesterday's dinner? Use them as flavoring. Raw vegetables can also be mixed in, but the flavor and consistency will be smoother using cooked ingredients.

LEGUMES	SEED/NUT BUTTERS	1–2 FLAVORINGS
Chickpeas	Tahini	Roasted or raw root vegetables: carrots or beets
White beans, large and small	Almond butter	Garlic: raw or roasted until soft
Yellow peas	Hazelnut butter	Turmeric
Green peas	Peanut butter	Spice mixes
Red lentils	Cashew butter	Fresh herbs
Yellow lentils	Cold-pressed olive oil	Sun-dried tomatoes
Fava beans	Cold-pressed canola oil	Grilled bell peppers
		Truffle oil

1–3 VEGETABLES

One of my favorite uses for leftovers, the last bit of a salad, or a few roasted root vegetables, is to sprinkle them over the bowl. This is a great way to make a feast out of scraps. Go ahead and mix the vegetables with a bright dressing before placing them on top of the hummus base.

LEAFY GREENS

A handful of mixed leafy greens, massaged cabbage leaves, or a handful of chopped fresh herbs provide a lively addition during the warmer months. Arrange them on the side, mix the vegetable leftovers with chopped herbs, or dress the leafy greens with a dressing of your choice for a fun variety.

1–2 TOPPINGS

This is the last piece of the puzzle—a crunchy or other inspiring ingredient to top off the hummus! We've also included dressings here. If you have a pre-cooked grain you want to add for a more nutritious dish, it goes here, too. Check out toppings from other recipes, too, as they work well here!

1–3 Vegetables	Leafy Greens	1–2 Toppings
Broccoli	Spinach	Toasted nuts or seeds
Red, pointy (also bulls-head/sweetheart) or white cabbage (oven-baked or massaged)	Mâche	Nut and kale sprinkles
	Arugula	Sauerkraut
	Romaine lettuce	Fresh herbs
Parsnip	Frisé lettuce	Bread and cabbage crumbs
Carrot	Chard shoots	Chickpea croutons or marinated legumes
Pumpkin	Cabbage shoots: kale, Tuscan cabbage	Cabbage chips
Zucchini	Massaged cabbage: kale, Tuscan cabbage, Brussels sprouts	Salt mixes
Mushrooms		Cooked grains
Tomato	Fresh herbs	
Cauliflower	Sprouts and shoots	
Garden peas		
Fennel		

THESS SUGGESTS

A hummus bowl is my favorite go-to preparation when I wanted food 5 minutes ago; very few meals are so quickly put together. You'll mix a hummus in a blink of an eye, and then cover it with different, more or less filling, toppings suitable for the occasion. It is also an excellent way to use up leftovers and those forgotten vegetables in the bottom of the refrigerator. A tasty crisp cracker or a slice of bread is always welcome.

	LEGUMES		SEED/NUT BUTTERS		1–2 FLAVORINGS
1.	Chickpeas	⟶	Light tahini	⟶	Ground turmeric
2.	Chickpeas	⟶	Tahini	⟶	Pesto rosso (see recipe on page 109) or sun-dried tomatoes
3.	Red lentils	⟶	Peanut butter	⟶	Garlic
4.	White beans	⟶	Almond butter	⟶	Parsley
5.	Garden peas	⟶	Tahini	⟶	Mint + lemon

1. Turmeric-flavored hummus topped with roasted carrots, cauliflower, toasted almonds, and pesto rosso (sun-dried tomato pesto)
2. Pesto rosso-flavored hummus topped with roasted pumpkin, kale, wild rice, and golden cashews
3. White bean hummus with almond butter and herbs, topped with baked tomatoes, eggplant, and julienned garden peas
4. Garden pea hummus with mint and lemon, topped with tomato salsa, yogurt, and chickpea croutons

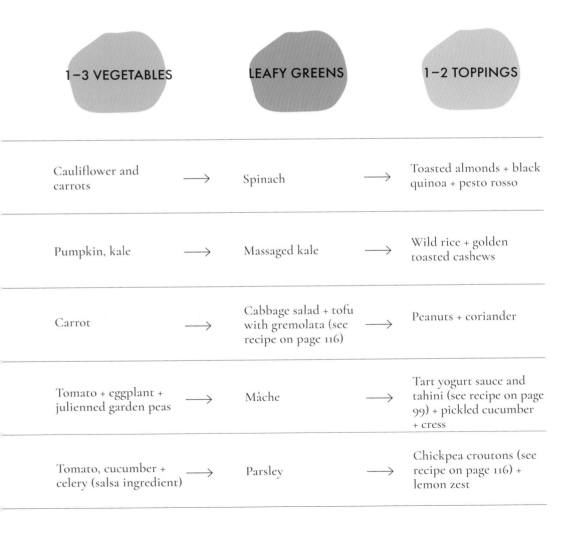

1–3 VEGETABLES		LEAFY GREENS		1–2 TOPPINGS
Cauliflower and carrots	$\longrightarrow$	Spinach	$\longrightarrow$	Toasted almonds + black quinoa + pesto rosso
Pumpkin, kale	$\longrightarrow$	Massaged kale	$\longrightarrow$	Wild rice + golden toasted cashews
Carrot	$\longrightarrow$	Cabbage salad + tofu with gremolata (see recipe on page 116)	$\longrightarrow$	Peanuts + coriander
Tomato + eggplant + julienned garden peas	$\longrightarrow$	Mâche	$\longrightarrow$	Tart yogurt sauce and tahini (see recipe on page 99) + pickled cucumber + cress
Tomato, cucumber + celery (salsa ingredient)	$\longrightarrow$	Parsley	$\longrightarrow$	Chickpea croutons (see recipe on page 116) + lemon zest

Everybody should be able to rattle off a basic recipe for hummus—and most importantly, mix it—even if they're awakened in the middle of the night. Hummus isn't just a base for bowls but also a way to impart creaminess, fullness, protein, and flavor in a lot of different dishes. It works as a sandwich and wrap filler and as accompaniment for salads. Hummus is also a dip for crunchy vegetable sticks, can be used as a pizza layer, and goes so well with a burger. And these are just a few ideas off the top of my head!

Classic hummus is made from chickpeas, but to get some variety, I make hummus from other legumes and still, playfully, continue to call it hummus. Here is the base recipe for hummus that will become your family standby. It is important to: 1) use light tahini, which is made from raw sesame seeds, and the consistency is slightly runnier and milder tasting than dark tahini, and 2) mix tahini and water first before you add the chickpeas and seasonings. That way your hummus will turn out soft and smooth!

BASE RECIPE FOR HUMMUS

½ lb (drained) precooked legumes—approx. 2 cups

Use the equivalent weight/volume in cooked yellow peas or frozen (but defrosted) garden peas. Cook ¾ cup red lentils for one batch hummus, and drain well before mixing. You don't need to add any extra liquid to the red lentils.

Ingredients
¼ cup water
2 tbsp light tahini
1 x 1½ lbs cooked, drained chickpeas
juice and zest from 1 organic lemon
salt flakes

How to: In a blender, mix the water and tahini. Rinse the legumes, but save one tablespoon of the chickpea liquid to add to the mix for extra volume! Add the rinsed legumes and blend until your preferred consistency— smooth or chunky. Season with salt and perhaps some flavorings.

Suggested flavorings
1) 2 handfuls of mixed fresh herbs plus grated garlic
2) 1 handful roasted carrots, beets, or pumpkin
3) 1 roasted bell pepper and 2 sun-dried tomatoes
4) ½ cup sauerkraut
5) 1 whole roasted bulb garlic plus 5 fresh French tarragon leaves
6) Ground turmeric, ginger, and ground cumin

PORRIDGE

1–2 kinds of cereals + liquid + 1–2 flavorings
fresh fruit or berries + 1–2 toppings

These are anytime meals. Yes, you read that right. Porridge is so much more than that meal with sweet toppings at breakfast. Think of porridge as a form of risotto—a creamy base topped with nutritional goodies, and as suitable for brunch as it is for a quick dinner. Try cooking porridge from whatever grain takes your fancy: oat, rye, spelt, sorghum/millet, or quinoa. If it is a more filling porridge you're after, add some grated carrot, beet, or zucchini and let them cook down with the grains until velvety. When you discover a grain that you especially like, mix up a bigger batch and store in a jar. That way, you can simply help yourself the next time you want to make some porridge. Add a splash of plant-based beverage and the mix will be extra smooth. I sometimes sprinkle dried flower petals on my porridges, simply for decorative purposes (only certain flower petals are edible), because they look so very pretty!

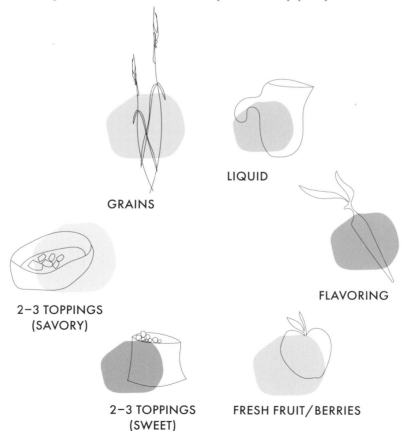

GRAINS

LIQUID

FLAVORING

2–3 TOPPINGS
(SAVORY)

2–3 TOPPINGS
(SWEET)

FRESH FRUIT/BERRIES

TIP COLUMN

Fruit and berry compote

In a saucepan, barely cover fruit of your choice with water, and cook them until soft. Then mash them slightly. Add a pinch of salt. If you like, add a pinch of ground cinnamon, ginger, cardamom, or vanilla powder. The compote will keep in the refrigerator for at least 3 days. It freezes well, too. This is a great way to save apples that are turning floury or have developed dark spots.

Nut and seed sauces

Blend equal parts of nut or seed butter, water, and a pinch of salt until the mixture turns creamy.

Here is another essential recipe to always keep close at hand—a basic porridge! Firm or creamy? It is wholly up to you, but the recipe below shows you how to start. Once you've cooked your porridge, just top it with a sweet or savory topping according to the formula.

PORRIDGE, BASIC RECIPE

<u>Each quantity makes 1 serving of warm porridge:</u>

2 ½ fl oz rolled oats (preferably soaked overnight) + 1 ½ cups liquid
½ cup oat flakes/spelt grains/barley grains + 1 ½ cups liquid
2 ½ fl oz millet (sorghum) flakes + 1 ½ cups liquid
½ cup whole quinoa + 1 ½ cups liquid

Cook the porridge until soft. Grains will need about 3 minutes. Crushed whole oats and quinoa will need about 15 to 20 minutes. Try mixing different grains, for example, 2 ½ fl oz rolled oats + ⅛ cup quinoa flakes, for a different effect. Add the toppings by following the formula.

<u>For 1 serving overnight (cold) porridge you'll need:</u>

½ cup rolled oats + 1 tbsp chia seeds + 1 cup plant-based beverage + ½–1 tsp flavoring/spice mixture like ground cinnamon, cardamom, or an Indian turmeric latte spice mix.

Go ahead and make a double or triple batch to keep in the refrigerator for several future breakfasts. Use toppings according to the formula.

<u>For 1 serving overnight (cold) buckwheat porridge you'll need:</u>

½ cup soaked (overnight) whole buckwheat + ½ cup berries + ¼ cup plant-based beverage + 1 tbsp nut, almond or seed butter + 1–2 flavorings, for example lemon, ginger, mint, or dates.

After soaking overnight, rinse the buckwheat to completely remove the gelatinous coating. Repeat this every morning if you have soaked a larger batch to use for several days. Blend all ingredients until smooth. Add a date if you want a sweeter porridge.

THE ULTIMATE FORMULA: PORRIDGE

1–2 GRAINS

Cereal grains are the porridge stars. Try mixing several kinds of grains to get new variations. A good tip to remember is that whole or crushed grains, like whole quinoa or steel-cut oats, provide more chewing satisfaction.

LIQUID

This is either water or a plant-based beverage—or a mixture of the two. If prepared overnight, the result will be tastier if the major part of the liquid is plant-based. The preparation will be extra creamy, especially with the addition of a spoonful of plant yogurt.

1–2 FLAVORINGS

Grate some carrot, beet, and/or zucchini into the porridge for more flavor and mouthfeel. Even a quick kiss of warming spices will impart delicious flavor.

1–2 GRAINS	LIQUID	1–2 FLAVORINGS
Crushed (steel cut) oats	Water	Indian turmeric latte (see recipe on page 101)
Rolled oats	Oat milk	Cinnamon
Quinoa flakes (good to mix with other grains/flakes)	Almond milk	Ginger
Sorghum (millet) flakes	Coconut milk	Turmeric
Spelt flakes	Soy milk	Fennel seeds
Amaranth	Pea milk	Pumpkin spice mix (see recipe on page 100)
Whole quinoa		Carrots
Mixed crushed grains: oats, rye, barley, and spelt		Beets
		Zucchini

FRESH FRUIT/BERRIES

Top with raw fruit or cook the fruit down, with a splash of water, or into a plain compote. Flavor the compotes with cinnamon, ginger, and cardamom.

Apples

Strawberries

Cranberries

Blueberries

Plums

Fruit and berry compotes

Pears

Chia seed jams

Blackberries

Raspberries

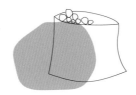

1–2 TOPPINGS (SWEET)

There are no restrictions here. Go ahead, take 5 toppings if that's what you feel like! Granola is a good choice when you want plenty of toppings, but it has to be quick to prepare—it'll include several of the suggestions below!

Granola, toasted seeds and nuts

Plant-based beverage or plant-based yogurt

Nut and seed butter

Coconut flakes

Dried flower petals (make sure you do your research to ensure you only consume those that are safe)

Cacao nibs

Fudgy date sauce (blend some fresh dates with a splash of water + a pinch of salt to a sweet fudge sauce)

Dried fruit or berries

Libyan Chraime sauce

1–2 TOPPINGS (SAVORY)

A more nutritious porridge means more savory toppings. Perhaps, in the beginning, these ingredients feel a bit unconventional, but I think you'll warm up to them. There are no restrictions on the amount here, either; go ahead and use as many as you wish!

Massaged kale or Tuscan cabbage

Vine-ripe garden tomatoes

Roasted root vegetable

Chickpea croutons

Avocado

Roasted Brussels sprouts or red cabbage

Plant-based yogurt

Squash

Apple

Toasted seeds and nuts

THESS SUGGESTS

My life changed (for real!) the day I found out that porridge wasn't just the world's most scrumptious breakfast, but I could also have it as a quick lunch or simple dinner. Since that revelation I eat porridge nearly daily, all year round! I have prepared a vast amount of different porridges using different grains and vegetables, and a multitude of flavorings. My Nordic soul is at peace when I stand at the stove and stir my porridge. Here are some favorites born from these times!

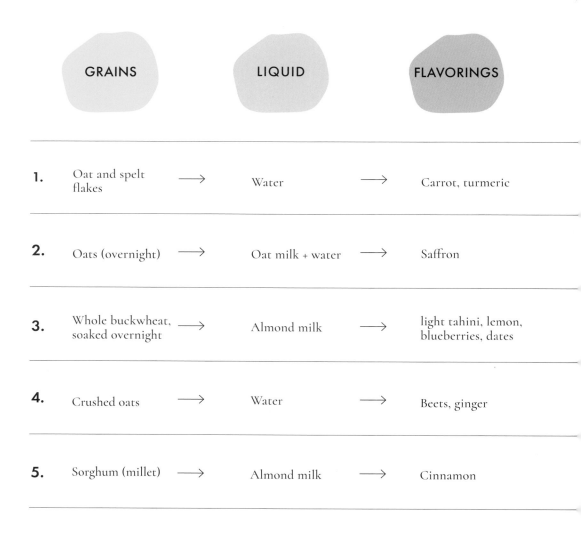

	GRAINS		LIQUID		FLAVORINGS
1.	Oat and spelt flakes	⟶	Water	⟶	Carrot, turmeric
2.	Oats (overnight)	⟶	Oat milk + water	⟶	Saffron
3.	Whole buckwheat, soaked overnight	⟶	Almond milk	⟶	light tahini, lemon, blueberries, dates
4.	Crushed oats	⟶	Water	⟶	Beets, ginger
5.	Sorghum (millet)	⟶	Almond milk	⟶	Cinnamon

1. Nutritious oat-spelt porridge with cranberries and apple compote, kale, mushrooms, and walnuts
2. Overnight oatmeal with saffron, cranberries, and apple compote, almond butter, and skimmed oat milk
3. Raw buckwheat porridge with blueberries, lemon, toasted walnuts, and plant-based yogurt
4. Crushed oat porridge with beets, ginger, apple, and granola
5. Cinnamon-scented sorghum porridge with strawberry compote, peanut butter, cacao nibs, and mint

FRESH FRUIT/BERRIES		1–2 TOPPINGS (SWEET)		1–2 TOPPINGS (SAVORY)
Cranberry and apple compote	$\longrightarrow$	Toasted walnuts	$\longrightarrow$	Massaged kale, fried mushrooms, steamed broccoli
Cranberry and apple	$\longrightarrow$	skimmed oatmilk + almond butter	$\longrightarrow$	
Fresh berries, dried apricots	$\longrightarrow$	Toasted walnuts, plant-based yogurt	$\longrightarrow$	
Apple	$\longrightarrow$	Granola, plant-based yogurt	$\longrightarrow$	
Strawberry compote	$\longrightarrow$	Peanut butter, cacao nibs, mint	$\longrightarrow$	

ESSENTIALS—RECIPES

The recipes in this section of the book both enhance and simplify most dishes. Dressings, sauces, bread and crackers, exciting toppings, and anytime smoothies—they're all here. You'll even find that little extra that sometimes just makes the dish. These recipes are easily thrown together, perhaps in larger batches that you can store in the pantry, refrigerator, or freezer for several days, sometimes weeks—if they last that long, that is.

The essential recipes are divided into categories as shown below. The handy combinations on pages 68 to 95 are some examples of how you can best use them.

SAUCES AND DRESSINGS

SPICE AND SALT MIXES

DIPS

BREAD AND SOURDOUGH

TOPPINGS

SMOOTHIES

SAUCES AND DRESSINGS

It's no secret that nearly all dishes can be embellished with a delicious dressing. Why not make a double batch to have on hand for future use? Mix all sauce or dressing ingredients until smooth, then season with salt. Add more liquid if you prefer a thinner sauce or dressing. Each recipe makes about 1 cup.

TURMERIC AND TAHINI SAUCE

½ cup light tahini • ½ cup water • 1 tbsp tamari/soy sauce • 1 tsp turmeric, ground • 2 tsp apple cider vinegar • ½ tsp coconut sugar

PUMPKIN SEED VINAIGRETTE

¼ cup pumpkin seeds, toasted • ½ cup canola oil, cold-pressed • ¼ cup apple cider vinegar • Dijon mustard

VEGAN MAYONNAISE, BASIC RECIPE

½ cup chickpea liquid or ¼ cup organic soy milk • 1 tbsp apple cider vinegar • 1 tbsp Dijon mustard 1–1¼ cups canola oi

Blend liquid, vinegar, and mustard. While mixing, add the oil in a thin stream until you have a fluffy mayonnaise. Grated garlic, chili, tamari, herbs, or truffle oil are all great seasonings.

SMOOTH CHIMICHURRI

2 handfuls fresh parsley • ½ shallot, finely chopped • 2 garlic cloves, finely grated • ½ cup olive oil, cold-pressed • zest and juice from 1 organic lemon • ⅖ tsp chili flakes

TART YOGURT-TAHINI SAUCE

1 cup oat yogurt • 2 tbsp light tahini zest from 1 organic lemon • 1 tbsp lemon juice • 10 mint leaves, finely chopped

MISO DRESSING

2 tbsp dark or 4 tbsp light miso paste • 4 tbsp seed or nut butter (ex. peanut butter or light tahini) • 2 tbsp apple cider vinegar • 2 tbsp water • 2 tsp maple syrup • 2 tsp tamari

ALMOND SAUCE

2½ fl oz almond butter • ½ cup water • 1 small garlic clove, finely grated • 1 tbsp nutritional yeast [not brewer's yeast] • 2 tsp apple cider vinegar • 1 tsp maple syrup

LIBYAN CHRAIME SAUCE

3 tbsp tomato puree • 2 tbsp apple cider vinegar • 2 tbsp olive oil, cold-pressed • 2 tbsp water • 1 tsp caraway seeds • 1 tsp paprika powder ½ tsp cinnamon, ground • 1 garlic clove, finely grated

SPICE AND SALT MIXES

Many regions the world over acted as inspiration for my spice and salt mix collection below. The spice mixes can be used both as seasoning in a dish, or sprinkled over the top. The salt mixes are mostly used as toppings. However, there's nothing wrong with rolling falafel or turning the vegetable burgers in a salt mix before frying or oven-baking them. Go ahead and pair the mixes with your preferred curry; most grocery stores have a large selection. This is a very simple way to vary dishes and also to simplify meal preparation. To prepare the spice and salt mixes, collect the ingredients, mix them, and store in airtight containers. Each recipe makes about ½ cup.

NORTH AMERICAN PUMPKIN SPICE MIX

4 tbsp cinnamon, ground • 2 tbsp ginger, ground • 1 tsp cloves, ground • 1 tsp nutmeg, ground

Good with: porridge, pumpkin soup, dressings, toasted nuts and seeds, pumpkin pie latte, muffins, and cookies.

MEXICAN TACO MIX

2 tbsp cumin seeds, ground • 1 tbsp coriander seeds, ground • 1 tbsp paprika powder • 2 tsp turmeric, ground • 2 tsp onion powder 2 tsp garlic powder • 2 tsp salt • 2 tsp oregano • ⅕ tsp chili powder—optional • ⅕ tsp black pepper

Good with: tacos —use as seasoning for ground soy meat, tempeh, tofu, or mushrooms.

LEVANTINE ZA'ATAR

1 tbsp sesame seed, with hulls • 2 tbsp sumac • 1 tbsp dried thyme • 1 tbsp dried marjoram • 1 tsp dried oregano 1 tsp salt flakes • 1 tsp onion powder

Good with: yogurt sauces, roasted vegetables; to mix with oil and drizzle over bread and pizza.

FRESH MEDITERRANEAN MIX

4 tbsp pine nuts • 3 tbsp fennel seeds • 4 tbsp toasted buckwheat (Tip section with "how to" on page 101) • 1 tbsp salt flakes

Chop the pine nuts coarsely. Crush the fennel seeds with mortar and pestle. Toast it all in a dry frying pan for a few minutes until there is a rich toasty smell. Let cool. Mix in buckwheat and salt flakes.

Good with: salads, sandwiches, yogurt sauces, hummus, grilled summer vegetables.

JAPANESE FURIKAKE

2 tbsp seaweed crumbs • 2 tbsp nutritional yeast [not brewer's yeast] • 2 tbsp sesame seed, with hulls • 1 tbsp black sesame seeds • 1 tsp onion powder • ½ tbsp salt flakes

If you can't find seaweed crumbs, just crumble a nori sheet. Nori is usually used for making sushi.

Good with: Sprinkle over a hearty sandwich; roll falafel or tofu in the mix before oven-baking, or sprinkle the mix over tofu salads.

INDIAN TURMERIC LATTE MIX

4 tbsp turmeric, ground • 1 tbsp cinnamon, ground • 1 tbsp ginger, ground • 1 tbsp cardamom, ground • ½ tsp black pepper, freshly ground • 1 tsp coconut sugar—optional

Good with: vegetable-beverage-based turmeric latte, toasted nuts and seeds, cold or warm porridge.

NORTH AFRICAN DUKKA

¼ cup walnuts, toasted and finely chopped • ¼ cup hazelnuts [filberts], skins removed, toasted and finely chopped • 2 tbsp sesame seeds, with hulls, toasted • 1 tbsp coriander seeds • 1 tbsp caraway seeds • 1 tbsp cumin seeds • ½ tbsp salt flakes

Toast coriander and cumin seeds in a medium hot frying pan for about one minute. Process the seeds to a coarse blend. Mix in nuts, sesame seeds, and salt flakes.

Good with: Good as hummus topping, sprinkled over roasted root vegetables, adding crunch to salads, or mixed with olive oil to dip sourdough bread in.

NORDIC WINTER MIX

1 ¾ oz kale leaves • 1 tsp oil • ½ cup hazelnuts [filberts], skins removed 2 tsp maple syrup • ½ tbsp salt flakes • ¼ cup dried cranberries

Chop the kale into smaller pieces and massage them with oil. Roast the kale in a 300°F (150°C) oven until the kale is crisp. Let cool and then crumble the pieces. Chop the hazelnuts coarsely, then mix them with maple syrup and salt flakes. Fry the nut mixture until the nuts are caramelized, then remove them to a plate and let cool. Mix in the dried cranberries and salt flakes.

Good with: salads, sandwiches, hummus, and in sourdough wraps.

TIP COLUMN

·

How to dry berries

Preheat the oven to 125°F (50°C). Place berries in a single layer on a parchment-covered baking sheet. Dry in the middle of the oven overnight, or until the berries are dry. Wedge a kitchen towel between the oven door and stove to allow the steam to escape during the drying.

How to toast buckwheat

Bring water to boil in a saucepan, then add dried whole buckwheat. Immediately remove the saucepan from the heat and drain the water. Rinse the buckwheat thoroughly and let it drain. Toast the buckwheat in a medium-hot frying pan or in an oven set at 300°F (150°C) until the buckwheat is dry and crunchy.

TIP COLUMN

How to tell the difference between light and dark tahini

Light tahini is made from raw sesame seeds and is very smooth with a mild flavor. Dark tahini is made from toasted sesame seeds, and the flavor is rather strong. Light tahini is best for dressings and sauces, while dark tahini is very nice spread on bread or as filling for dried fruit.

DIPS

Depending on how they are used, these dips serve approximately four to eight people. The carrot dip is good as a mash with the coconut-breaded tofu (see recipe on page 115), falafel, or whatever takes your fancy. Make a double batch to have plenty of mash for four people. All the dips will keep for at least four days if refrigerated, so go ahead and mix up larger batches for future use.

WHITE BEAN DIP WITH ROASTED GARLIC AND PARSLEY

1 small head of garlic • oil • 8 oz white beans, cooked, drained weight • 2 tbsp olive oil, cold-pressed 1 bunch fresh parsley • salt flakes

Preheat the oven to 395°F (200°C). Peel off the garlic's papery outer layer and brush the bulb with oil. Bake the garlic until soft, about 30 minutes. Let the garlic cool and then squeeze out the cloves. Blend the cloves with the white beans, cold-pressed olive oil, and parsley until completely smooth. Season with salt.

BABA GHANOUSH WITH LOADS OF LEMON

2 eggplants • 2 tbsp oil • 2 tbsp light tahini paste • zest and juice from 1 organic lemon • 1 garlic clove, finely grated • 10 fresh mint leaves • salt flakes

Preheat the oven to 395°F (200°C). Slice the eggplants into approximately ⅓" (cm) rounds. Brush the cut surfaces with plenty of oil. Place the slices on a baking sheet and roast in the oven for about 25 minutes. Turn the slices over halfway through the roasting. Remove the peel (it can be finely chopped and spread over the prepared dip). Use a food processor to blend the eggplant meat with the tahini, lemon, garlic, and 10 mint leaves. Season with salt and pepper.

OVEN-BAKED CARROT DIP/ CUSTARD WITH MISO AND GINGER

10½ oz of carrots • 1 tsp oil • ½ tsp dark (or 1 tsp light) miso paste • 1 tbsp ginger, freshly grated • 1 tbsp canola oil, cold-pressed • salt flakes

Preheat the oven to 395°F (200°C). Clean the carrots thoroughly. Cut them into smaller pieces and brush them with oil. Place the pieces on a baking sheet and roast in the oven until they are soft, approx. 40 minutes. Blend them together with the miso paste, ginger, and cold-pressed olive oil until they are a smooth consistency. Add some water if you want a thinner dip. Season with salt.

GREEN PEA-TSATSIKI

9 oz (250 gr) green peas, frozen • 2 tbsp olive oil, cold-pressed (+ extra for serving) • ½ cup plant-based yogurt (full fat) • 1 small garlic clove, finely grated • zest and juice from 1 organic lemon, • 1 bunch fresh basil salt flakes • black pepper, freshly ground

Defrost the peas. Blend all the ingredients to smooth dip. Season with salt and pepper.

BREAD

Bread is the perfect complement (and sometimes even the base) to plenty of dishes! I bake a few more quickly put-together varieties, in addition to sourdough bread. Here is something for the weekend brunch, picnic in the woods, and also for weekend snacking.

OAT SCONES WITH CARROTS

1¾ cups (4 dl) oat flour • 6¾ fl oz (2 dl) rolled oats • 2 tsp baking powder •
3 tbsp chia seeds • ½ tsp salt • 1 carrot, finely grated • 1 handful dried berries or fruit •
¼ cup (½ dl) oil • 6¾ fl oz vegan beverage

Preheat the oven to 440°F (225°C). Mix dry ingredients. Add thoroughly squeezed-out carrot and dried berries or fruit (your choice). Add oil and the plant-based beverage. Mix everything without kneading.

Place eight mounds on a baking sheet. Bake them for approximately 15 to 18 minutes, until they are slightly golden and the surface is crisp. Serve the scones with a sweet topping, a plant-based yogurt, and fruit or berry compote—or something more filling like avocado and sprouts.

POTATO FLATBREAD

1¾ lbs firm potatoes, cooked and cooled •
1 pinch salt flakes • 8½ fl oz oat flour • ½ cup oat flour or millet flakes for sprinkling

Finely grate the potatoes and mix with salt and oat flour to a dough. Separate into 8 parts. Sprinkle with oat flour or millet flakes and roll out into thin round flatbreads.

Fry the flatbreads in a dry frying pan over medium heat. Fry both sides until they are nicely colored. Fill the breads with delicious fillings for a rollup! PS: An afterthought—Try varying the bread flavor with, for example, herbs or garlic.

LENTIL CRACKERS

½ cup red lentils • ½ cup pumpkin seeds • ½ cup sunflower seeds • ¼ cup flax seeds • 3 tbsp psyllium husk • ½ tsp salt flakes • 1 cup boiled water • 2 tbsp canola oil, cold-pressed

Soak the lentils and seeds overnight—at least six hours. Rinse. Mix lentils and seeds with the rest of the ingredients. Let rest for 10 minutes. Place the mixture between two pieces of parchment paper. Roll out two thin sheets. Bake the sheets, one at a time, in the middle of an oven preheated to 350°F (175°C) for 30 minutes. Turn the sheet and bake for another 10 minutes. Repeat with the second sheet. Let cool and then break the sheets into smaller pieces.

TOPPINGS

Apart from being a shortcut to add a little something to all your dishes to make them special, toppings also solve the eternal problem of what to bring as gifts for the hostess. If you're already making some toppings, make an extra batch. Place it in an attractive jar and bring it to the next dinner party.

ALMOND FETA

3½ oz almonds, blanched • 2 tbsp apple cider vinegar • ¼ cup good-quality olive oil, cold-pressed • 1 tbsp nutritional yeast [not brewer's yeast] • 1 tsp salt flakes

Soak the almonds for at least 12 hours. Rinse the almonds. Mix the almonds with the rest of the ingredients until smooth and creamy. Place the mixture in cheesecloth or a clean kitchen towel and wring it hard to drain the liquid. Place the drained mixture in the refrigerator for at least 12 hours. Heat the oven to 260°F (125°C). Place the almond mixture on a baking sheet and flatten the mixture into an approximately ½" (1 cm) thick sheet. Bake for 30 minutes. Let cool. *Tips!* Try seasoning the mixture with dried herbs. The almond feta will keep at least one week in the refrigerator.

NUT AND KALE CRUMBS

3½ oz kale • 1 cup cashews • ¼ cup sesame seeds • 2 tbsp chia seeds 1 tbsp olive oil • 1 tsp maple syrup • 1 good pinch salt flakes

Preheat the oven to 305°F (150°C). Rinse the kale, remove the coarse stems (save them to use in the recipe on page 12), and chop the leaves to tiny pieces in a food processor. Add cashews, sesame seeds, chia seeds, olive oil, maple syrup, and salt flakes. Proceed to make coarse crumbs. Roast the crumbs on a baking sheet, stirring occasionally, about 30 minutes until they are dry and crisp.

SPICE PICKLED MUSHROOMS

9 oz portabella mushrooms • ¼ cup apple cider vinegar • ¼ cup tamari • ¼ cup water, boiling • 1 tbsp fresh ginger, grated • ⅕ tsp cardamom, ground

Finely shred the mushrooms and place them in a bowl. Mix the rest of the ingredients. Pour the liquid over the mushrooms and let them rest at least one hour, but stir now and then. Save and use the pickling liquid for another batch of mushrooms!

HERBY CASHEW RICOTTA

3½ oz organic cashews • 1 tbsp lemon juice, freshly squeezed • ¼ cup good-quality olive oil, cold-pressed • 1 tbsp nutritional yeast [not brewer's yeast] • 1 small garlic clove, finely grated • a few branches fresh thyme • 1 tsp salt flakes

Soak the cashews overnight, or at least four hours. Rinse them. Mix the cashews with the rest of the ingredients into a grainy ricotta-like texture. The cashew ricotta will keep at least one week in the refrigerator.

PESTO ROSSO

3½ oz tomatoes, sun-dried • ½ cup pumpkin seeds • 1 tbsp nutritional yeast [not brewer's yeast] • ½ cup good-quality olive oil, cold-pressed • 1 handful of fresh parsley • ½ small garlic clove, finely grated • 1 tsp coconut sugar

Soak the tomatoes in boiling water for 10 minutes. Drain the tomatoes. In a food processor blend the tomatoes together with pumpkin seeds, nutritional yeast, olive oil, fresh parsley, finely grated garlic, and coconut sugar into a flavorful pesto. Season with salt.

SMOOTHIES

What's the greatest invention since sliced bread? If you ask me, it's smoothies. Because they can be made savory or sweet, they're the perfect replacement for any meal. They're ideal for when you're on the go and variations are limitless. To please vegetable-rejecting children (and adults, too), just add some greens to a smoothie and disguise it with, for example, sweet and berry-flavored ingredients. Smoothies are quick to prepare, too! I use organic produce whenever possible and blend the whole vegetables (lemons with their peel; fresh, unpeeled ginger; entire apples; and kale, complete with the hard stem—just to mention some). I'll remove the thicker peel from some citrus, like oranges, but mix in the zest.

Using a powerful blender will turn out a silky smoothie in under a minute. The instructions are simple: mix everything until smooth and then prepare add-ins to individual taste. For a fluid smoothie, add more liquid. If you prefer a sweeter smoothie, put in some freshly pitted dates. To make it more filling, include soaked buckwheat or rolled oats. Use less liquid to get a thicker smoothie bowl. All recipes are enough for 2 glasses.

STRAWBERRY—PEANUT BUTTER—GINGER— LEMON

7 oz strawberries, frozen • 2 tbsp peanut butter • ¾" fresh ginger, thoroughly cleaned • ½ organic lemon, peel intact • ½ cup buckwheat, dried whole—soaked at least 8 hours or overnight, thoroughly rinsed • 2 cups oat milk, another plant-based beverage, or water

GREEN PEA—FENNEL—APPLE—LEMON

1 cup green peas • 2 stalks celery • ½ head fennel • 1 red apple • 1 large handful organic spinach or kale • ½ organic lemon with peel intact • 2 fresh dates, pits removed • 2 cups pea liquid, another plant-based beverage, or water

MIXED BERRIES—BEETROOT—CAULIFLOWER—GINGER

7 oz mixed berries • 1 beetroot, thoroughly cleaned • 5¼ oz cauliflower, frozen • 2 tbsp light tahini • ¾" fresh ginger, thoroughly cleaned • ½ organic lemon, peel intact • 2 cups oat milk, another plant-based beverage, or water

CARROT—SEA BUCKTHORN—ORANGE—ALMOND BUTTER

2 carrots • 3½ oz sea buckthorn, frozen • 1 organic orange, peeled • 2 tbsp almond butter • 2 fresh dates, pits removed • 2 cups oat milk, another plant-based beverage, or water

DIFFERENT WAYS WITH VEGETABLE PROTEINS

Page 47 explains how the vegetable world is full of protein. More or less everything you eat contains different amounts of protein. On the following page spread you'll find suggestions for preparing and using three plant-based ingredients that contain abundant amounts of protein and are easy to dish up and serve. The purpose of this section is to give you the resources, found within these recipes, to modify many different dishes. You can make them more filling and also more protein-rich for the occasions when you need this—like when you are very active or if you're athletic.

Remember, there exist numerous additional high-value protein sources beyond these, for example: all kinds of legumes, seeds, nuts, and cereals.

Depending on how central they are to the whole meal and how they will be used, the recipes will serve 4 to 6 people. At the end, you'll also find a recipe for absolutely divine chocolate balls made with a secret ingredient—chickpeas!

ROASTED CHIMICHURRI TOFU

1 lb 2 oz tofu, firm • 1 tsp oil • ½ cup chimichurri dressing (recipe on page 99) • salt flakes

Dice the tofu. Fry the pieces in oil in a medium-hot frying pan until they are golden all over. Place the tofu in a bowl and fold it into a smooth chimichurri dressing. Season with salt. Serve in a salad, in a wrap, or serve the fried tofu and dressing as part of a buffet.

RED ONION AND APPLE VEGAGEN [*]

9 oz tofu, firm • 1 tsp oil • 1 cup vegan yogurt, full fat • ¼ cup vegan mayonnaise (or ¼ cup vegan yogurt) • 2 tbsp seaweed caviar • 2 tbsp dill, finely chopped • zest and juice from 1 organic lemon • 1 red apple, finely chopped • ½ red onion, finely chopped • salt flakes • black pepper, freshly ground

Crumble the tofu and fry it in some oil until the crumbs are golden. Remove the pan from the heat and place the crumbs in a bowl. Mix the vegan yogurt, vegan mayonnaise (see page 99), seaweed caviar, dill, lemon, red apple, and red onion. Mix, and season with salt and freshly ground black pepper. This tastes delicious with crackers and sourdough!

* After Skagen Salad, a Swedish seafood salad

COCONUT-BREADED TOFU

3 tbsp tamari • 3 tbsp apple cider vinegar • 1 tbsp ginger, freshly grated • 1 lb 2 oz tofu, firm • ½ cup vegan mayonnaise • ½ cup coconut, grated

Mix tamari, apple cider vinegar, and ginger into a marinade. Slice the tofu and place it in the marinade for 20 minutes; turn the pieces after 10 minutes. Heat the oven to 395°F (200°C). Dip the tofu slices in the mayonnaise and then in the grated coconut. Place the slices on a baking sheet and roast them in the middle of the oven for about 20 minutes. Let the tofu cool some. Serve with the almond sauce from page 99. *Tip!* The marinade can be used as a base for a nut, almond, or seed dressing.

TOFU SCRAMBLE WITH SUN-DRIED TOMATOES AND PARSLEY

1 small yellow onion • 1 tsp oil • 9 oz tofu, firm • 1 tbsp nutritional yeast [not brewer's yeast] • ½ tsp turmeric, ground • 2 sun-dried tomatoes, finely shredded • 2 tbsp plant-based beverage or water • 2 tsp tamari • 1 handful parsley, chopped • salt flakes • black pepper, freshly ground

Brown the onion in a frying pan. Add a teaspoon of oil and crumble in the tofu. Fry until the tofu is slightly golden. Sprinkle the nutritional yeast, turmeric, and sun-dried tomatoes over the tofu. Add the plant-based liquid and tamari and let it soak in. Remove from the heat. Mix in the parsley and season with salt and freshly ground pepper. This is the perfect lunch meal or every day dinner that is ready in a jiffy. Prepare a double batch if it is to be served as the only dish. Serve with good bread.

"SCRAMBLE" PIE

9 oz tofu, silken • 1 cup plant beverage • 2 tbsp nutritional yeast [not brewer's yeast] • ½ tsp salt flakes • ⅕ tsp black pepper, freshly ground

In a blender, or using an immersion blender, mix the silken tofu, plant beverage, nutritional yeast, salt and black pepper until smooth. Pour the mixture into a pre-baked pie shell filled with your favorite vegetables. Bake for 35 to 45 minutes at 395°F (200°C) until the mixture has settled and is lightly golden. Let cool slightly before serving.

TOFU

HERBY CHICKPEA SCRAMBLE WITH LEMON

1 lb chickpeas, cooked, drained weight • zest and juice of ½ organic lemon • 2 tbsp nutritional yeast [not brewer's yeast] • ½ tsp turmeric, ground ½ tsp garlic powder • 1 tsp oil • 2 tbsp light tahini • 4 tbsp water • 1 handful parsley, finely chopped • ⅕ tsp chili flakes • salt flakes • black pepper, freshly ground

Drain and rinse the chickpeas. Mash them with the lemon, nutritional yeast, turmeric, and garlic until they are a coarse mix. Fry the mix in some oil for a few minutes. Whisk together tahini and water. Add the tahini and parsley to the chickpeas to make a creamy scramble. Add some more water if the scramble feels too dry. Season with salt and pepper.

CHICKPEAS IN GREMOLATA MARINADE

2 large handfuls of parsley • 20 fresh mint leaves—optional, but they add an interesting touch • zest and juice of 1 organic lemon • 1 clove garlic, finely grated • ¾ cup olive oil, cold-pressed • 1 lb chickpeas, cooked, drained weight • salt flakes

Finely chop the parsley and mint leaves. Mix them with lemon, garlic, and cold-pressed olive oil and season with salt. Drain and rinse the chickpeas then mix with the desired amount of gremolata. *Tip!* The gremolata can be used as dressing or marinade for other dishes like tempeh, tofu, or prepared vegetables—or as a dip for sourdough bread!

OVEN-BAKED CARROT FALAFEL WITH BASIL

1 lb chickpeas, cooked, drained weight • 1 ½ cups carrots, finely grated and squeezed dry • 2 handfuls basil, fresh or 2 tbsp frozen • 1 small garlic clove, finely grated • 1 tsp cumin, ground • ½ tsp salt

Preheat the oven to 395°F (200°C). Drain and rinse the chickpeas and make a flavorful mix together with carrot, fresh basil (or 4 tablespoons frozen), garlic, cumin, and salt. Form into approximately 20 balls and roll them in sesame seeds. Place the balls on a baking sheet and bake for about 15 minutes. Turn the balls over and bake for another 10 to 15 minutes until the falafel is crisp.

CHICKPEA CROUTONS

½ lb chickpeas, cooked, drained weight • ½ tbsp olive oil • ½ tsp paprika • ½ tsp whole caraway seeds • ⅕ tsp garlic powder • 1 pinch salt flakes

Preheat the oven to 350°F (175°C). Drain and rinse the chickpeas, and dry them with a towel. Mix the chickpeas with olive oil, paprika, cumin, garlic, and salt flakes. Place the mix on a baking sheet. Roast in the oven for about 10 minutes until the chickpea mix is crisp and golden. This works equally well with white beans.

CHOCOLATE BALLS WITH A SECRET INGREDIENT

14 fresh dates, pits removed • ½ lb chickpeas, cooked, drained weight • ½ cup cocoa powder • ½ cup peanut butter • 1 big pinch salt flakes • dark chocolate or cacao to cover

In a food processor, mix the ingredients until smooth. Roll the mixture into approximately 16 balls. If you want to, dip the balls in melted chocolate and let them set. They are also delicious when rolled in cocoa or grated coconut (melted chocolate is optional). Store the balls preferably in the freezer, as they are delicious when properly chilled.

CHICKPEA

TEMPEH

TEMPEH IN TERIYAKI MARINADE

½ cup tamari • ½ cup water • 2 tbsp apple cider vinegar • 2 fresh dates, pits removed • 2 garlic cloves, finely grated • 1 tbsp fresh ginger, finely grated • 1 lb 2 oz tempeh

In a blender, mix the tamari, water, vinegar, fresh dates, garlic, and ginger until smooth. Cube or slice the tempeh and marinate it for at least 15 minutes. Heat the oven to 395°F (200°C). Place the tempeh on a baking sheet. Roast the tempeh in the middle of the oven for about 10 minutes. Turn the tempeh over and at the same time brush it with the marinade. This is good served with furikake (see recipe on page 100).

SWEET 'N SPICY PEANUT TEMPEH

1 lb 2 oz tempeh • 2½ fl oz peanut butter • ½ cup tamari • 2½ fl oz apple cider vinegar • 1 tbsp maple syrup • 3 tbsp water • ⅗ tsp chili flakes

Cube the tempeh. Mix peanut butter, tamari, vinegar, maple syrup, water, and chili flakes until smooth. Cover the tempeh with marinade and let rest at least 20 minutes. Heat the oven to 395°F (200°C).

Bake the tempeh on a baking sheet for about 15 minutes, turning it over after half the time. Mix the tempeh with the rest of the marinade.

FALAFEL MADE WITH TEMPEH, MINT, AND SUNFLOWER SEEDS OR NUTS

1 lb 2 oz tempeh • 1 shallot, finely chopped • 1 garlic clove, finely grated • 1 tbsp fresh ginger, grated • 1 cup seeds or nuts, toasted • 1 handful fresh parsley • 1 tbsp olive oil, cold-pressed

Blend tempeh, shallot, garlic, ginger, toasted seeds or nuts, fresh parsley, and cold-pressed olive oil until smooth. Make 20 falafel shapes, and roll them in sesame seeds. Place the falafels on a baking sheet. Heat the oven to 350°F (175°C). Bake the falafel for 20 minutes, turning them over after half the time, until they are slightly crisp on the outside.

TACO-LIKE GROUND TEMPEH

1 lb 2 oz tempeh • 1 tsp oil • 2 to 3 tbsp Mexican Taco Mix (see recipe on page 100) • ¼ cup vegetable beverage

Crumble or grate the tempeh. In an oiled pan, fry the tempeh until it is slightly browned all over. Sprinkle the tempeh with the Mexican Spice Mix and pour in the vegetable liquid. Stir to combine everything. Fry another minute and then serve inside tacos!

CONVERSION CHARTS

Metric and Imperial Conversions
(These conversions are rounded for convenience)

Ingredient	Cups/Tablespoons/Teaspoons	Ounces	Grams/Milliliters
Butter	1 cup/ 16 tablespoons/ 2 sticks	8 ounces	230 grams
Cheese, shredded	1 cup	4 ounces	110 grams
Cornstarch	1 tablespoon	0.3 ounce	8 grams
Cream cheese	1 tablespoon	0.5 ounce	14.5 grams
Flour, all-purpose	1 cup/1 tablespoon	4.5 ounces/0.3 ounce	125 grams/8 grams
Flour, whole wheat	1 cup	4 ounces	120 grams
Fruit, dried	1 cup	4 ounces	120 grams
Fruits or veggies, chopped	1 cup	5 to 7 ounces	145 to 200 grams
Fruits or veggies, pureed	1 cup	8.5 ounces	245 grams
Honey, maple syrup, or corn syrup	1 tablespoon	0.75 ounce	20 grams
Liquids: cream, milk, water, or juice	1 cup	8 fluid ounces	240 milliliters
Oats	1 cup	5.5 ounces	150 grams
Salt	1 teaspoon	0.2 ounce	6 grams
Spices: cinnamon, cloves, ginger, or nutmeg (ground)	1 teaspoon	0.2 ounce	5 milliliters
Sugar, brown, firmly packed	1 cup	7 ounces	200 grams
Sugar, white	1 cup/1 tablespoon	7 ounces/0.5 ounce	200 grams/12.5 grams
Vanilla extract	1 teaspoon	0.2 ounce	4 grams

Oven Temperatures

Fahrenheit	Celsius	Gas Mark
225°	110°	¼
250°	120°	½
275°	140°	1
300°	150°	2
325°	160°	3
350°	180°	4
375°	190°	5
400°	200°	6
425°	220°	7
450°	230°	8

INDEX—RECIPES

Did you try the thought experiment on page 7? Great! Here are my suggestions:

• Carrot soup with quinoa, apple, and chickpea salad topping, kale chips and vegan aioli

• Carrot falafel with saffron-scented quinoa, baked apples, and herby yogurt sauce

• Quinoa salad with marinated chickpeas, massaged kale, pickled apple, and yogurt-tahini dressing

INDEX—INGREDIENTS

THANK-YOUS

My warmest thank-yous to all of you who have, in different ways, made this book possible: The Book Affair's Alexandra Lidén, Alexandra Torstendahl, and Gabriella Sahlin for your knowledge and kindness. You believed in my idea from the first moment, pepped me all along the process, and offered your invaluable input, professionalism, and your genuine workmanship; and simply because you helped me turn *Plant-Based Cooking for Absolute Beginners* into reality.

Gaia Padovan for unbeatable design concept and illustrations; also to Lisa Kullberg for her fantastic design—I am so very happy to have been able to do this together with you. The inspiring Agnes Maltesdotter for wonderful photos, and to Elin Dahlström for great assisting. To Andreas Olsson, who let us use his magical kitchen; and to my mom, who assisted, tested recipes, and generally helped.

Many thank-yous to all those friends and family who have listened, tasted, given your opinions, and answered questions—you are invaluable!

And perhaps, most of all, thanks to all of you who hold this book in your hands. Together we will reach out to everyone with plant-based cooking, make vegetables cool, legumes sexy, and of course, prepare really delicious food!

My thanks also go to Electrolux® because you believed in my idea—and wanted to participate in spreading plant-based inspiration the world over. For *better living. Designed in Sweden.*

With its roots firmly anchored in Sweden and a sustainable relationship with nature and the environment, Electrolux® works toward solutions for better daily—and future—living. They have made sure that, for the last hundred years, produce is kept fresher longer, food preparation is simple and accessible, and importantly, all kinds of produce can be prepared with precision. Electrolux®'s designs are made to help people live better, less complicated lives. Giving them time to explore more. Each and every day. This goes hand-in-hand with my dream of making a plant-based cuisine people-friendly, more accessible, sustainable, and delicious. That's why I am so very grateful that Electrolux® wanted to join in this book project.